INTRODUCTION

Welcome to the *Precepts For Living® Personal Study Guide!* When using it, we hope that you will find it to be an enlightening and rewarding experience. This study guide can be used as a reference tool for any teacher or student who is serious about learning and knowing the inspired Word of God. It is designed to be used in conjunction with the *Precepts For Living® Annual Commentary*. It should help you get the God-intended meaning of each Scripture presented and explained in *Precepts*. Therefore, it is suggested that you use the guide in the following way:

- First thoroughly study each lesson of *Precepts*.

- Then go to the companion lesson in this study guide and answer all the questions pertaining to the lesson.

- After you have answered all of the questions for a particular lesson **on your own**, check your answers by using the **Answer Keys** that are found in the back of the book.

- If you miss an answer, go back and research it in *Precepts*. This will enhance both your learning experience and memorization of Scripture.

Enjoy this *Precepts For Living® Personal Study Guide*. As you do your Bible study, observe Scripture, grasp it by correctly interpreting the text, and then walk in the knowledge of God's Word.

TABLE OF CONTENTS

PRECEPTS FOR LIVING® PERSONAL STUDY GUIDE

UMI MISSION STATEMENT: *We are called of God to create, produce, and distribute quality Christian education products; to deliver exemplary customer service; and to provide quality Christian educational services, which will empower God's people, especially within the Black community, to evangelize, disciple, and equip people for serving Christ, His kingdom, and church.*

Precepts For Living® Personal Study Guide, Vol. 2, No. 1, September 2006–August 2007. Published yearly by UMI (Urban Ministries, Inc.), P.O. Box 436987, Chicago, IL 60643-6987. Founder and Chairman: Melvin E. Banks Sr., Litt.D.; President and CEO: C. Jeffrey Wright, J.D. ; Director of Editorial: Cheryl Clemetson, Ph.D.; Writer: Evangeline Carey; Designer: Trinidad D. Zavala. Lessons based on International Sunday School Lessons; the International Bible Lessons for Christian Teaching. Copyright© 2003 by the Committee on the Uniform Series. Used by permission. Supplementary Lesson Development. Copyright© 2006 by UMI. All rights reserved. **$37.95** per copy (postage included). Printed in the U.S.A. **NO PART OF THIS PUBLICATION MAY BE REPRODUCED IN ANY FORM WITHOUT THE WRITTEN PERMISSION OF THE PUBLISHER.**

To order: Contact your local Christian bookstore; call UMI at 1-800-860-8642; or visit our website at www.urbanministries.com.

TABLE OF CONTENTS

PRECEPTS FOR LIVING® PERSONAL STUDY GUIDE

GOD'S COVENANT WITH NOAH

> "And I will remember my covenant, which is between me and you and every living creature of all flesh; and the waters shall no more become a flood to destroy all flesh" (Genesis 9:15).

GENESIS 9:1–15

Use with Bible Study Guide 1.

MORE WORDS AND PHRASES

Match the following words or phrases with the correct definitions.

1. _____ covenant

2. _____ a reminding symbol of God's promise

3. _____ a peace bond made between God and humanity

4. _____ what blood symbolizes

5. _____ God spoke directly to them

a. rainbow

b. Noah and his sons

c. a binding agreement

d. token

e. life

JUMP-STARTING THE LESSON

6. In the IN FOCUS story, what was the great tsunami that rolled over Jean's life?

_____

7. What reassurance did God send Jean to remind her of His grace? _____

_____

UNDERSTANDING THE LESSON

8. The Noahic covenant was unilateral and unconditional in the sense that God initiated it and guaranteed it with action on the part of humankind (see THE PEOPLE, PLACES, AND TIMES).   True   False

9. List six life experiences that could have caused Noah and his family doubt, fear, and insecurity.

a. _____

b. _____

c. _____

d. _____

e. _____

_____

f. _____

_____

10. List two different types of covenants.

a. _____

_____

_____

_____

b. _____

_____

_____

_____

_____

_____

11. In Genesis 9:1, God blessed Noah and his wife, and said, "Be fruitful, and multiply, and replenish the earth."
True   False

12. According to Genesis 9:2, "the fear of you (humanity) and the dread of you (humanity)" will include the
fowl of the air.   True   False

13. Man should not eat flesh (Genesis 9:3).   True   False

14. The blood of animals should not be eaten because all flesh was made in the image of God (Genesis 9:4).
True   False

15. When God said in Genesis 9:6, "Whoso sheddeth man's blood, by man shall his blood be shed," He
declared _____ punishment for any _____.

16. "The waters shall no more become a flood to destroy all flesh" (Genesis 9:15).

True   False

17. What makes the blood of animals and humans significant (Genesis 9:1–15)?

a. _____

b. _____

18. What does God mean in Genesis 9:15 when He says, "And I will remember my covenant, which is between me and you and every living creature of all flesh"?

_____

_____

_____

COMMITTING TO THE WORD

19. Explain how Genesis 9:1–15 is relevant to current issues in our society.

_____

_____

_____

_____

_____

WALKING IN THE WORD

20. Based on Genesis 9:1–15, how can we evaluate the candidates and elected officials who seek our votes?

_____

_____

_____

_____

_____

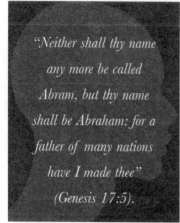

GOD'S COVENANT WITH ABRAM

"*Neither shall thy name any more be called Abram, but thy name shall be Abraham: for a father of many nations have I made thee*" (Genesis 17:5).

G E N E S I S   1 7 : 1 - 8 ,   1 5 - 2 2

Use with Bible Study Guide 2.

MORE WORDS AND PHRASES

Match the following names with the words or phrases that define them.

1. _____ Abraham   a. "he laughs"

2. _____ El Shaddai   b. Princess

3. _____ Abram   c. Hebrew for "Creator"

4. _____ Sarai   d. Almighty God

5. _____ Isaac   e. Exalted Father

6. _____ Elohim   f. a father of many nations

JUMP-STARTING THE LESSON

7. In the IN FOCUS story, before marriage, what was the understood covenant between Ken and Carmen?

_____

_____

8. List four things that challenged the covenant that Ken and Carmen made with each other.

a. _____

b. _____

c. _____

d. _____

UNDERSTANDING THE LESSON

9. God established His covenant with Abram and all of his descendants (Genesis 17:4).

True   False

10. What was the covenant that God made with Abraham (Genesis 17:5–6)?

_____

_____

_____

_____

_____

_____

11. Who did God promise to multiply exceedingly (Genesis 17:6, 20)?

a. Abraham

b. Sarah

c. Ishmael

d. Isaac

e. a and c

12. In Genesis 17:7–8, what were the three parts of the covenant that God made with Abraham?

a. _____

b. _____

c. _____

13. What was God's promise concerning Sarah (Genesis 17:16)?

a. _____

b. _____

c. _____

14. Explain how Sarah is a mother of nations (Genesis 17:16).

_____

_____

15. Why did God name Abraham and Sarah's future son "Isaac" (Genesis 17:17, 19)?

_____

_____

16. How old was Sarah when she gave birth to her son, Isaac (Genesis 17:17)?

a. 70   b. 80   c. 90   d. 100

17. What covenant did God establish with Ishmael (Genesis 17:20)?

_____

18. "But my _____ will I _____ with _____"

(Genesis 17:21).

COMMITTING TO THE WORD

19. What four things can you do to make faith initiatives in your life?

a. _____

b. _____

c. _____

d. _____

WALKING IN THE WORD

20. What can you do to encourage others to have faith in God?

_____

_____

_____

_____

GOD'S COVENANT WITH ISRAEL

EXODUS 19:1–6; 24:3–8

"And Moses came and told the people all the words of the LORD, and all the judgments: and all the people answered with one voice, and said, All the words which the LORD hath said will we do" (Exodus 24:3).

Use with Bible Study Guide 3.

MORE WORDS AND PHRASES

Match the words or phrases with the correct definitions.

1. _____ judgment

2. _____ eagle's wings

3. _____ covenant

4. _____ holy

5. _____ obey

a. a binding agreement

b. set apart

c. formal decree

d. to fully follow instructions

e. symbol of God's care and deliverance

JUMP-STARTING THE LESSON

6. In the IN FOCUS story, how did Minister John biblically define our Christian "covenant" with God?

_____

_____

_____

7. How did Minister John see our Christian relationship with God?

_____

_____

8. What did Minister John see as part of our covenant responsibility?

_____

_____

_____

7

UNDERSTANDING THE LESSON

9. Of all the nations in the world, the _____

were chosen by God to be His _____ peo-

ple (see THE PEOPLE, PLACES, AND TIMES).

10. Name three things God did to redeem the Israelites
(Exodus 19:4).

a. _____

_____

b. _____

_____

c. _____

11. What two things did God require the Israelites to do (Exodus 19:5)?

a. _____

b. _____

12. Why was being God's "peculiar treasure" such an honor and privilege for the Israelites (Exodus 19:5)?

_____

_____

_____

_____

13. The Israelites were to be a kingdom of princes (Exodus 19:6).   True   False

14. God comes to us as He came to Israel as _____ sovereign Lord, our

_____ (Exodus 24:3–8).

15. In Exodus 24:4, what was the significance of Moses building an altar?

_____

16. In Exodus 24:4, the twelve pillars represented the _____

_____.

17. The Book of the Covenant was the expanded and detailed version of the Decalogue, the _____

_____ (Exodus 24:7, see IN DEPTH).

COMMITTING TO THE WORD

18. List *one* covenant or contract you entered, and note how you felt when the other party breached the

covenant or contract. _____

_____

_____

_____

_____

19. List *one* covenant or contract you have breached, and note how you plan on recommitting to it (if possible).

_____

_____

_____

WALKING IN THE WORD

20. Honestly assess why it is difficult for you to keep some of your promises and fulfill certain covenants. List

these pitfalls and some ways that you can become more committed to the covenants you enter.

_____

_____

_____

_____

> "And if it seem evil unto you to serve the LORD, choose you this day whom ye will serve; whether the gods which your fathers served that were on the other side of the flood, or the gods of the Amorites, in whose land ye dwell: but as for me and my house, we will serve the LORD" (Joshua 24:15).

COVENANT RENEWED

J O S H U A   2 4 : 1 ,   1 4 – 2 4

Use with Bible Study Guide 4.

MORE WORDS AND PHRASES

Match the names with the phrases that define them.

1. _____ Amorites
2. _____ the LORD
3. _____ Joshua said,
4. _____ elders, judges, and officers
5. _____ God is
6. _____ the Israelites said,

a. "But as for me and my house, we will serve the LORD."
b. holy and jealous
c. "The LORD our God will we serve."
d. The LORD drove them out of the land.
e. helped Israel to renew their commitment
f. brought the Israelites out of Egypt

JUMP-STARTING THE LESSON

7. In the IN FOCUS story, what did Shelia mean, in terms of Debra's salvation, when she asked Debra, "Do you want to *fly* or *fry?*" _____

_____

_____

8. Shelia told Debra that "accepting and serving the Living God is a _____."

UNDERSTANDING THE LESSON

9. Before Joshua's death, the call to covenant renewal was significant because it:

a. reminded the people that Joshua was not their "real" leader, but just a servant of God

b. made it clear that Joshua's death should *not* be the end of Israel's commitment to God

c. encouraged the people to choose for themselves to serve God

d. all of the above

10. Where did Joshua and the leaders gather (Joshua 24:1)? _____

11. Why did Joshua gather the people together (Joshua 24:1)? _____

_____

_____

12. When Joshua told the Israelites "to fear the Lord," what did he mean (Joshua 24:14)?

_____

_____

_____

13. What did Joshua mean when he told the Israelites to "serve him (God) in sincerity and in truth" (Joshua 24:14)? _____

_____

14. Joshua reminded the Israelites that it is their choice to choose evil or to choose God (Joshua 24:15).
True   False

15. What three reasons did Joshua give for the nation's inability to serve God (Joshua 24:19)?

a. _____

b. _____

c. _____

16. Every covenant should be held as sacred and witnessed. If there are no witnesses, there is no accountability for the parties involved (Joshua 24:22).   True   False

17. Joshua called the Israelites witnesses _____ _____ (Joshua 24:22).

18. Demonstration of faith in the God of the covenant was required by the single but hard action of putting away their idols (Joshua 24:23).   True   False

COMMITTING TO THE WORD

19. The Israelites had to put away the gods of other nations. What "gods" are in your life that you must relinquish to serve God fully?

_____

_____

_____

WALKING IN THE WORD

20. Renewing one's covenant with God begins with a choice to repent and then serve God. Commit or recommit to your covenant with God by first repenting of sin and telling God of your decision. Now list at least two people who you will share your choice with. Then pray that God will provide the opportunity for you to share your covenant renewal story with each person.

a. _____

b. _____

GOD SENDS JUDGES

"Nevertheless the LORD raised up judges, which delivered them out of the hand of those that spoiled them" (Judges 2:16).

J U D G E S   2 : 1 6 - 2 3

Use with Bible Study Guide 5.

MORE WORDS AND PHRASES

Match the words with the correct definitions.

1. _____ spoiled   a. refusing to yield, obey, or comply

2. _____ deliver   b. to keep down by the cruel or unjust use of power or authority

3. _____ groan   c. a nation or force hostile to another

4. _____ judge   d. to overstep or break a law, commandment, etc.

5. _____ enemy   e. stripped of goods, money, etc. by force

6. _____ oppress   f. to set free or save from evil, danger, or restraint

7. _____ stubborn   g. a governing leader in Israel after Joshua and before King Saul

8. _____ transgress   h. to utter a deep sound expressing pain, distress, or disapproval

JUMP-STARTING THE LESSON

9. In the IN FOCUS story, what was Lena's cycle of rebellion against God?

_____

_____

UNDERSTANDING THE LESSON

10. The judges were _____ leaders, who _____ raised in times of crisis to

_____ _____ from the hand of its enemies (see THE PEOPLE, PLACES, AND

TIMES).

11. The recurring pattern of Israel's rebellion included: apostasy, _____, moaning

by the Israelites, and their subsequent _____ and _____ (see BACKGROUND).

12. Instead of listening to their judges, what three things did the Israelites do (Judges 2:17)?

a. _____

_____

b. _____

_____

c. _____

_____

13. When the Lord raised up judges to deliver the people, how long was there peace in the land before they repeated the cycle (Judges 2:18)? _____

_____

14. The people cried out to the Lord because (Judges 2:18):

 a. They were repentant.

 b. They were tired of being oppressed.

 c. They loved the Lord.

15. After the judge died, the Israelites continued to do as the Lord commanded (Judges 2:19).
True   False

16. The Israelites had a legacy of _____ adultery (Judges 2:19).

17. The Lord was angry with the people because (Judges 2:20):

a. They disobeyed His covenant.

b. They ignored His voice.

c. They married foreigners.

d. all of the above

18. The Lord tested the nation of Israel to see whether or not they would keep the commandments as their ancestors did (Judges 2:22).   True   False

COMMITTING TO THE WORD

19. The Lord heard the groans of the Israelites and took pity on them. Can you recall a time when you cried out to God and He answered your prayers?

_____

_____

_____

_____

_____

_____

WALKING IN THE WORD

20. Identify some young people with whom you can share the story of God's saving grace through examples of the Israelites' deliverance from Egypt, their deliverance from the hand of their enemies in Canaan, or your personal testimony. Write down what you will tell them.

_____

_____

_____

_____

_____

_____

_____

> "And Barak said unto her, If thou wilt go with me, then I will go: but if thou wilt not go with me, then I will not go. And she said, I will surely go with thee: notwithstanding the journey that thou takest shall not be for thine honour; for the LORD shall sell Sisera into the hand of a woman. And Deborah arose, and went with Barak to Kedesh" (Judges 4:8–9).

GOD LEADS THROUGH DEBORAH

JUDGES 4:4-10, 12-16

Use with Bible Study Guide 6.

MORE WORDS AND PHRASES

Match the names or places with the correct definitions.

1. _____ Deborah a. Galilean tribe called upon to battle Sisera

2. _____ Barak b. the captain of Jabin's army

3. _____ Jabin c. husband of Deborah

4. _____ River Kishon d. judge and prophetess in Israel

5. _____ Sisera e. lofty place from where Barak led the charge against Sisera

6. _____ Lapidoth f. king of Canaan

7. _____ Abinoam g. location of battle between Barak's troops and Sisera's army

8. _____ Naphtali h. father of Barak

9. _____ Mount Tabor i. military commander of Israel's army

JUMP-STARTING THE LESSON

10. In the IN FOCUS story, how did Lawrence, in the film *Lawrence of Arabia,* demonstrate the leadership quality of serving? _____

_____

11. What did Lawrence mean by the words, "Nothing is written unless you write it"?

_____

_____

UNDERSTANDING THE LESSON

12. Deborah was the mother of Barak (Judges 4:4).

True   False.

13. Deborah was a _____ (Judges 4:4).

a. judge

b. prophetess

c. military leader

d. all of the above

14. The Lord commanded Barak to _____ (Judges 4:6).

a. go to Mount Tabor

b. go to Mount Ephraim

c. go to the Kishon River

15. How many troops did the Lord instruct Barak to gather (Judges 4:6)? _____

16. The Canaanites had _____ iron chariots (Judges 4:6–10).

a. 400   b. 500   c. 700   d. 900   e. 1000

17. In Judges 4:9, what was the significance of Deborah's prediction that "the Lord shall sell Sisera into the hand of a woman"?

a. _____

b. _____

18. Who was actually fighting for Israel (Judges 4:14)? _____   _____

COMMITTING TO THE WORD

19. Sisera saw his "state-of-the-art" army annihilated by the lesser forces of the Israelites. The defeat of the Canaanite army demonstrated that no matter how overwhelming the forces in our life appear, God can vanquish them. Recount a situation in your life that appeared impossible to overcome, but God delivered you.

WALKING IN THE WORD

20. Just like Barak, we sometimes negotiate with God before agreeing to do His will. List the "if/then" conditions you have set with God, and resolve today to submit to His will.

GOD ANSWERS SAMUEL'S PRAYER

1 SAMUEL 7:3-13

"And Samuel took a sucking lamb, and offered it for a burnt offering wholly unto the LORD: and Samuel cried unto the LORD for Israel; and the LORD heard him" (1 Samuel 7:9).

Use with Bible Study Guide 7.

MORE WORDS AND PHRASES

Match the names with the correct definitions.

1. _____ Samuel   a. "stone of help"

2. _____ Ashtaroth   b. prophet, priest, and judge

3. _____ Ebenezer   c. conquered the Israelites

4. _____ Philistines   d. consort of Baal; false god

5. _____ Mizpeh   e. change of mind; turn from sin to God

6. _____ repent   f. place where Samuel prayed for the Israelites

JUMP-STARTING THE LESSON

7. In the IN FOCUS story, what did Tamara's family do for her while she was away?

_____

UNDERSTANDING THE LESSON

8. The Israelites needed to repent and return to God (1 Samuel 7:3–7).   True   False

9. What were Samuel's three roles (1 Samuel 7:3–13)?

a. _____ b. _____ c. _____

10. What had the Israelites done that angered God (1 Samuel 7:3–4)?

_____

11. What four things did Samuel urge the Israelites to do (1 Samuel 7:3–4)?

a. _____

_____

b. _____

_____

c. _____

_____

d. _____

12. What happened at Mizpeh (1 Samuel 7:5)? _____

_____

13. What is "intercessory prayer" (1 Samuel 7:5–6)? _____

_____

14. What did the Philistines do when they heard that the Israelites had gathered at Mizpeh (1 Samuel 7:7)? Why? _____

_____

_____

15. What did the Israelites ask Samuel to do for them when they realized the Philistines were attacking (1 Samuel 7:8)? _____

16. What was God's response to Samuel and the Israelites' cry for help (1 Samuel 7:10)?

_____

_____

17. What did Samuel name the stone that he set between Mizpeh and Shen (1 Samuel 7:12)?

_____

18. The hand of the LORD was *with* the Philistines all the days of Samuel (1 Samuel 7:13)?

True   False

COMMITTING TO THE WORD

19. Share your personal experience of the power of prayer (when you prayed for yourself or when someone

interceded for you). _____

_____

_____

_____

_____

WALKING IN THE WORD

20. Write a prayer asking God to strengthen your prayer life. _____

_____

_____

_____

_____

_____

"And thine house and thy kingdom shall be established for ever before thee: thy throne shall be established for ever" (2 Samuel 7:16).

GOD COVENANTS WITH DAVID

2 S A M U E L 7 : 8 – 1 7

Use with Bible Study Guide 8.

MORE WORDS AND PHRASES

Match the words, phrases, or names with the correct definitions.

1. _____ David

a. a prophet, David's personal advisor

2. _____ Ish-bosheth

b. capital of Judah

3. _____ seed

c. serves as a symbol of the presence of God

4. _____ Nathan

d. Saul's son, who was king of the rest of Israel at the time David was crowned king of the tribe of Judah

5. _____ Jerusalem

e. a descendant or an offspring

6. _____ Ark of the Covenant

f. king of all Israel

JUMP-STARTING THE LESSON

7. In the IN FOCUS story, how had Greg's mother and father's broken promise to each other cause Greg to stumble? _____

_____

_____

UNDERSTANDING THE LESSON

8. David wanted to bring the Ark of the Covenant to Jerusalem to ensure God's blessings upon the nation of Israel (2 Samuel 7:8–17)?   True   False

9. Why did David want to build a temple for the Ark of the Covenant (2 Samuel 7:8–17)?

_____

_____

_____

_____

10. What did God want David to do (2 Samuel 7:8)?

_____

_____

11. God's plans for Israel were _____ (2 Samuel 7:10).

a. a place of their own

b. a place where they would not have to move anymore

c. their enemies would not afflict them anymore

d. all of the above

12. Both David and God wanted David to build a house for God (2 Samuel 7:11)?   True   False

13. What is the Davidic Covenant (2 Samuel 7:12–16)? _____

_____

14. With which son of David would God establish a kingdom (2 Samuel 7:12)? _____

15. How long would the lineage or house of David last (2 Samuel 7:13)? _____

16. The Davidic kingdom is bound to their covenant with God (2 Samuel 7:15).   True   False

17. Within the Davidic Covenant, what three things did God promise David would endure forever (2 Samuel 7:16)? a. _____ b. _____ c. _____

18. The prophet who represented God to David was _____ (2 Samuel 7:17).

a. Nathan   b. Moses   c. Jeremiah   d. Elijah

COMMITTING TO THE WORD

19. There are many promises in the Bible that God has given His children. List some of them.

_____
_____
_____
_____

WALKING IN THE WORD

20. Society encourages us to pursue materialism, pride, and recognition. If your major plan for your life needed to be changed because it was not God's will for you, would you be obedient to God? Explain why or why not. _____

_____
_____
_____

GOD GRANTS WISDOM TO SOLOMON

1   K I N G S   3 : 3 – 1 4

> *"Behold, I have done according to thy words: lo, I have given thee a wise and an understanding heart; so that there was none like thee before thee, neither after thee shall any arise like unto thee"*
> *(1 Kings 3:12).*

Use with Bible Study Guide 9.

MORE WORDS AND PHRASES

Use the list of biblical words to fill in the blanks below.

a. honour

b. Solomon

c. statutes

d. child

e. pleased

f. Gibeon

1. "And _____ loved the LORD, walking in the statues of David his father: only he sacrificed and burnt incense in high places" (1 Kings 3:3).

2. "And the king went to _____ to sacrifice there; for that was the great high place: a thousand burnt offerings did Solomon offer upon that altar" (1 Kings 3:4).

3. "And now, O LORD my God, thou hast made thy servant king instead of David my father: and I am but a little _____: I know not how to go out or come in" (1 Kings 3:7).

4. "And the speech _____ the LORD, that Solomon had asked this thing" (1 Kings 3:10).

5. "And I have also given thee that which thou hast not asked, both riches, and _____: so that there shall not be any among the kings like unto thee all thy days" (1 Kings 3:13).

6. "And if thou wilt walk in my ways, to keep my _____ and my commandments, as thy father David did walk, then I will lengthen thy days" (1 Kings 3:14).

JUMP-STARTING THE LESSON

7. In the IN FOCUS story, what did Michael do to help his wife, Liz, to get renewed confidence?

_____

_____

8. Relating the story to King Solomon, Solomon also

_____ and asked God for

_____ and _____ to

receive the wisdom God has promised to give us through

_____.

UNDERSTANDING THE LESSON

9. Solomon's ascent to the throne was marked by

_____ in David's household (1 King 3:3, see IN DEPTH).   a. peace   b. turmoil

10. Solomon's relationship with God was based on _____ teaching him who Jehovah was (1 King 3:3).

11. Solomon offered sacrifices to God in the temple of Jerusalem (1 Kings 3:4).   True   False

12. How many burnt offerings did Solomon sacrifice upon the altar to God (1 Kings 3:4)?
a. 50   b. 100   c. 500   d. 1000

13. Solomon's dream was a _____ visitation from the Lord (1 Kings 3:5).

14. Solomon had great confidence in his ability to lead the people (1 Kings 3:7).   True   False

15. When Solomon referred to himself as a "little child" in 1 Kings 3:7, what did he mean?

_____

_____

_____

16. Solomon knew that the people he was to lead belonged to _____ (1 Kings 3:8–9).

17. Solomon asked God to give him an understanding _____ to judge God's people, that he (Solomon) may _____ between _____ and _____ (1 Kings 3:9).

18. God promised Solomon that if he would _____ in God's _____, keep His _____ and _____ as his father David did, then God would _____ the days of Solomon's life (1 Kings 3:14).

COMMITTING TO THE WORD

19. Give two examples of how believers today can walk in God's ways and keep His statutes.

a. _____

b. _____

WALKING IN THE WORD

20. List several ways that you can apply godly wisdom in your personal everyday life.

a. _____

b. _____

c. _____

ELIJAH TRIUMPHS WITH GOD

"And when all the people saw it, they fell on their faces: and they said, The LORD, he is the God; the LORD, he is the God" *(1 Kings 18:39).*

1 KINGS 18:20-24, 30-35, 38-39

Use with Bible Study Guide 10.

MORE WORDS AND PHRASES

Use the list of biblical words to fill in the blanks below.

a. halt   b. repaired   c. spoken   d. Ahab   e. twelve   f. prophet

1. "So _____ sent unto all the children of Israel, and gathered the prophets together unto mount Carmel" (1 Kings 18:20).

2. "And Elijah came unto all the people, and said, How long _____ ye between two opinions? if the LORD be God, follow him: but if Baal, then follow him. And the people answered him not a word" (1 Kings 18:21).

3. "Then said Elijah unto the people, I, even I only, remain a _____ of the LORD; but Baal's prophets are four hundred and fifty men" (1 Kings 18:22).

4. "And call ye on the name of your gods, and I will call on the name of the LORD: and the God that answereth by fire, let him be God. And all the people answered and said, It is well _____" (1 Kings 18:24).

5. "And Elijah said unto all the people, Come near unto me. And all the people came near unto him. And he _____ the altar of the LORD that was broken down" (1 Kings 18:30).

6. "And Elijah took _____ stones, according to the number of the tribes of the sons of Jacob, unto whom the word of the LORD came, saying, Israel shall be thy name" (1 Kings 18:31).

JUMP-STARTING THE LESSON

7. According to the IN FOCUS, we should wait until we feel powerful or confident to take the first step of faith.

True   False

8. God releases His power before we take the first step of faith.   True   False

UNDERSTANDING THE LESSON

9. King Ahab was king of the _____ kingdom of Israel and was Israel's _____ king (see THE PEOPLE, PLACES, AND TIMES).

10. King Ahab was the first godly king of Israel to take a heathen wife (see MORE LIGHT ON THE TEXT).
True   False

11. King Ahab's wife was named _____ (see BACKGROUND).

12. King Ahab called the people together at Mount Carmel (1 Kings 18:20).   True   False

13. The people of Israel had a loud and angry response to Elijah's challenge that they choose who they would serve (1 Kings 18:21).   True   False

14. Circle the correct answer. There were how many prophets of Baal (1 Kings 18:22)?
a. 100   b. 250   c. 300   d. 400   e. 450

15. The stage was set for a spectacular demonstration of God's ability to _____ and_____ _____ Israel's _____ relationship with God (1 Kings 18:24, see IN DEPTH).

16. Elijah selected 12 stones representing who (1 Kings 18:31)? _____
_____

17. "The fire of the LORD fell, and _____ the burnt _____, and the

_____, and the _____, and the _____, and licked up the

_____ that was in the trench" (1 Kings 18:38).

18. When the people saw the handiwork of the Lord, they stood up and began to sing (1 Kings 18:39).
True   False

COMMITTING TO THE WORD

19. How do today's Christians "halt" or show indecisiveness about serving God?

_____

_____

_____

_____

WALKING IN THE WORD

20. In what ways are you challenging your unsaved friends, family members, and coworkers to choose to serve

God? _____

_____

_____

_____

JOSIAH BRINGS REFORM

2 KINGS 22:8-10; 23:1-3, 21-23

> "And the king stood by a pillar, and made a covenant before the LORD, to walk after the LORD, and to keep his commandments and his testimonies and his statutes with all their heart and all their soul, to perform the words of this covenant that were written in this book. And all the people stood to the covenant" (2 Kings 23:3).

Use with Bible Study Guide 11.

MORE WORDS AND PHRASES

Match the phrases with the correct names or words.

1. _____ purified Judah and Jerusalem from idolatry

2. _____ Josiah's great-grandfather

3. _____ Josiah's wicked father

4. _____ served as a channel through which God's blessings would flow

5. _____ "the book of the law of Yahweh" was by his hand

6. _____ an annual Hebrew festival commemorating

        the last meal in Egypt

a. Amon

b. Abraham

c. Moses

d. Passover

e. Hezekiah

f. Josiah

JUMP-STARTING THE LESSON

7. In the IN FOCUS story, what message did Pastor Duane want to demonstrate to his congregation?

_____

_____

_____

8. What recipe did Pastor Duane give the congregation for "fresh" spiritual bread each day?

a. _____ b. _____ c. _____

UNDERSTANDING THE LESSON

9. The three decades of Josiah's reign were characterized by peace, prosperity, and reform (see THE PEOPLE, PLACES, AND TIMES).   True   False

10. Josiah diligently sought the God of king _____ (see THE PEOPLE, PLACES, AND TIMES).

11. The book of the law of Yahweh contained

_____ of Yahweh. (see BACK-

GROUND).

12. The book of the law of Yahweh that was found was actually the "Mosaic book of the law," called the _____ (2 Kings 22:8–10, see IN DEPTH).

13. The book was lost under the idolatrous kings: _____ and _____ (2 Kings 22:8–10, see IN DEPTH).

14. Young king Josiah set out to repair what two things (see MORE LIGHT ON THE TEXT)?

a. _____

b. _____

15. Josiah means "_____" (see MORE LIGHT ON THE TEXT).

16. Josiah did more than repent when the law was read to him; he took action (2 Kings 23:1–3)!   True   False

17. Josiah began rebuilding the temple and returning worship to Yahweh at what age (see MORE LIGHT ON THE TEXT)?

a. 16   b. 20   c. 30   d. 45

18. The Passover was an important festival because it was a kind of sacrament, uniting the

_____ to _____ (2 Kings 23:21–23).

COMMITTING TO THE WORD

19. "And the _____ stood by a pillar, and made a _____ before the

_____, to walk after the _____, and to keep his _____ and

his _____ and his _____ with _____ their _____ and

_____ their _____, to perform the words of this covenant that were written in this book" (2 Kings

23:3).

WALKING IN THE WORD

20. What action do you need to take to reform your life and bring it into harmony with God's will? Write a

prayer expressing your situation to God. _____

_____

_____

_____

_____

_____

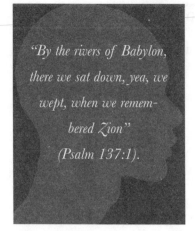

*"By the rivers of Babylon, there we sat down, yea, we wept, when we remembered Zion"
(Psalm 137:1).*

THE PEOPLE GO INTO EXILE

2 CHRONICLES 36:15—21; PSALM 137:1–6

Use with Bible Study Guide 12.

MORE WORDS AND PHRASES

Match the words, phrases, or names with the correct definitions.

a. temple   c. Jerusalem   e. Babylon   g. prophets

b. songs of Zion   d. Nebuchadnezzer   f. Zedekiah

1. _____ God's spokesmen, who often forewarned His people of judgment and doom

2. _____ a land in the farthest part of the Middle East where Israel was taken into captivity

3. _____ the ruler of Babylon, who was used by God to defeat His people

4. _____ the 21-year-old king, who ruled in Judah during the time of deportation of the
   Jews and destruction of the temple

5. _____ praise and worship that reminded the Jews of their homeland

6. _____ the city of God founded in peace

7. _____ the place where God's presence abides among His people

JUMP-STARTING THE LESSON

8. In the IN FOCUS story, what wrong choice did Mark make? _____

_____

9. What did Mark's wrong choice cost him? _____

_____

UNDERSTANDING THE LESSON

10. In 2 Chronicles 36:15, why was it necessary for God to send messengers to His people?

_____

_____

_____

_____

_____

_____

11. Why would God allow Nebuchadnezzar to destroy the temple and bring all of the precious and hallowed items to Babylon (2 Chronicles 36:15–17)?

_____

_____

12. In 2 Chronicles 36:16, what does the phrase "till there was no remedy" mean in light of today's lesson?

_____

_____

13. According to the prophet, how long would the children of Judah remain in Babylon (2 Chronicles 36:20–21, see **MORE LIGHT ON THE TEXT**)? _____

14. What is the relation between 2 Chronicles 36:15–21 and Psalm 137:1–6?

_____

_____

_____

15. Why was it difficult for the children of Judah to sing songs of Zion while being held captive in Babylon (Psalm 137:3–4)? _____

_____

16. It was evident from the attitude of the Jews that God had forsaken them while they lived in Babylon (Psalm 137:5).

True   False

17. What did the Jews mean by the statement, "if I prefer not Jerusalem above my chief joy" (Psalm 137:6)?

_____

_____

_____

_____

18. Circle the correct answer. What prophet did God use to declare His judgment on the people (see **MORE LIGHT ON THE TEXT**)?   a. Zephaniah   b. Isaiah   c. Jeremiah   d. Hosea

COMMITTING TO THE WORD

19. Today's lesson reminds us of the importance of confessing our sins and repenting of our wrong actions before the Lord. Share an experience where you failed to obey the Lord, and describe the consequences that disobedience had on your spiritual life. _____

_____

_____

_____

WALKING IN THE WORD

20. In light of today's lesson, list some ways to help others who may be struggling with sin issues in their lives.

_____

_____

_____

_____

GOD OFFERS RETURN AND RESTORATION

"Thus saith Cyrus king of Persia, All the kingdoms of the earth hath the LORD God of heaven given me; and he hath charged me to build him an house in Jerusalem, which is in Judah. Who is there among you of all his people? The LORD his God be with him, and let him go up" (2 Chronicles 36:23).

2 CHRONICLES 36:22–23; EZRA 1:5–7

Use with Bible Study Guide 13.

MORE WORDS AND PHRASES

Match the names or words with the correct definitions.

a. Cyrus   c. Levites   e. Persia   g. Jeremiah

b. offering   d. proclamation   f. Judah and Benjamin

1. _____ an official pronouncement or statement made by the king

2. _____ a large empire stretching from India to Greece that defeated the Babylonians, allowing the Jews to return to their homeland

3. _____ the king who threatened Babylonian rule and permitted the Jews to rebuild Jerusalem and its temple

4. _____ God's primary spokesperson during the fall of Jerusalem and the restoration of the exiles

5. _____ the two tribes that made up the southern kingdom of Israel

6. _____ those who served the priesthood and are considered as sons of Aaron

7. _____ the provisions the people brought to their leaders to help restore the temple

JUMP-STARTING THE LESSON

8. In the IN FOCUS story, had Pearl forgiven herself for her teen pregnancy and giving up her baby?

_____

9. Did Pearl feel that she had made the right decision and why? _____

_____

UNDERSTANDING THE LESSON

10. In 2 Chronicles 36:22, what was the "word of the Lord" that was spoken by Jeremiah (from IN DEPTH)?

_____

_____

_____

11. What did Cyrus mean when he said, "[God] hath charged me to build him an house in Jerusalem, which is in Judah" (2 Chronicles 36:23)?

_____

12. Cyrus declared that, "All the _____ of the _____ hath the LORD God of _____ given me" (2 Chronicles 36:23).

13. Who was responsible for starting the temple's construction in Jerusalem (Ezra 1:5)?

_____

_____

_____

14. What did the people bring to the leaders to help with the construction of the temple (Ezra 1:6)?

_____

_____

15. What was the greatest contribution given by Cyrus (Ezra 1:7)? _____

_____

16. God sometimes uses *unbelievers* to fulfill His destiny and purpose (Ezra 1:7, see IN DEPTH).

True   False

17. How were the people motivated to begin the work of restoring Jerusalem and the temple (see IN DEPTH)? _____

18. The importance of rebuilding the temple for the Jews was that it would return national pride and worship to Jerusalem (see MORE LIGHT ON THE TEXT).   True   False

COMMITTING TO THE WORD

19. Share a time when God used an unbeliever to help fulfill His purpose in your life.

_____

_____

_____

_____

_____

WALKING IN THE WORD

20. List some of the ways you have experienced compassion and forgiveness from the Lord so that you can demonstrate compassion and forgiveness to others.

_____

_____

_____

_____

_____

"Who is the image of the invisible God, the firstborn of every creature: For by him were all things created, that are in heaven, and that are in earth, visible and invisible, whether they be thrones, or dominions, or principalities, or powers: all things were created by him, and for him" (Colossians 1:15–16).

WHO IS JESUS CHRIST?

C O L O S S I A N S   1 : 1 5 – 2 3

Use with Bible Study Guide 1.

MORE WORDS AND PHRASES

Match the words or phrases with the correct definitions.

1. _____ Gnostics
2. _____ Redeemer
3. _____ Colossae
4. _____ sustain
5. _____ reconcile
6. _____ Saul of Tarsus
7. _____ an epistle
8. _____ Euphrates
9. _____ Ephesus

a. a letter
b. home of the Ephesians
c. one who ransoms or atones for another
d. believers of mystic philosophy
e. maintain, support, and keep alive
f. home of the Colossians
g. bring together, reunite, resolve
h. Paul
i. largest river in Western Asia

JUMP-STARTING THE LESSON

10. In the IN FOCUS story, what did Albert have to do to initiate reconciliation with his brother, Craig?

_____

_____

11. Paul writes to the Colossians that Christ is "the image of the invisible God." Use at least four different words that, for you, share the "image" of God (Colossians 1:15).

a. _____ c. _____

b. _____ d. _____

12. Explain the phrase, "Christ is supreme" (Colossians 1:15–19)? _____

_____

_____

_____

_____

13. Christ created and is before all thrones, dominions, principalities, and powers. According to Colossians 1:16–17, all things were created by Him and for Him. With so much confusion between different countries and their rulers, hatred, and wars; how can this be?

_____

_____

_____

14. Is each one of the principalities and powers acting on God's behalf? Explain. _____

_____

_____

15. Are the confusion, hatred, and wars relevant to whether or not Christ created the principalities and powers and is before them? _____

_____

_____

16. Why do you think "it pleased the Father that in Him should all fullness dwell" (Colossians 1:19)?

_____

_____

17. Before his conversion, Saul of Tarsus was wholly devoted to destroying Christians. Do you think after his conversion, Paul could have impacted the world as he did without first being Saul of Tarsus?

_____

_____

_____

18. From Colossians 1:15–23, list at least four attributes of God.

a._____ c. _____

b. _____ d. _____

COMMITTING TO THE WORD

19. Paul's past and Christ's redemption were useful motivators for Paul's new path, which included: beatings, prison sentences, and eventually losing his head under Nero's rule? Consider your past and tell how God has used it to make you an effective witness for Him.

_____

_____

_____

_____

_____

WALKING IN THE WORD

20. Can you think of anything painful in your past that could be put to good use for Christ?

_____

_____

_____

_____

_____

WHAT GOD SAYS ABOUT JESUS

H E B R E W S   1 : 1 – 9

> *"God, who at sundry times and in divers manners spake in time past unto the fathers by the prophets, Hath in these last days spoken unto us by his Son, whom he hath appointed heir of all things, by whom also he made the worlds" (Hebrews 1:1–2).*

Use with Bible Study Guide 2.

MORE WORDS AND PHRASES

Match the names or phrases with the correct definitions.

1. _____ the Trinity   a. the Bible

2. _____ the Canon   b. the superior Priest and Sacrifice

3. _____ the Apocrypha   c. God, the Father; God, the Son; God, the Holy Spirit

4. _____ Jesus   d. where books not put in the Canon were placed

5. _____ the Word of God   e. the accepted books of the Bible

JUMP-STARTING THE LESSON

6. List two reasons why the IN FOCUS poem says that we should celebrate Jesus.

a. _____

b. _____

7. Because of who Christ is, we should give him the highest _____,

our highest _____, and our highest _____ (see IN FOCUS poem).

UNDERSTANDING THE LESSON

8. It is clear that Paul wrote the book of Hebrews.   True   False

9. Hebrews was written for Greeks.   True   False

10. Hebrews is often referred to as the "fifth gospel."   True   False

11. Gnosticism is not a problem today.   True   False

12. Hebrews explains Christ's deity.   True   False

13. Jesus is superior to the prophets and the angels.   True   False

14. The nature of Christ is all important to the discussion of salvation.   True   False

15. God spoke to His people in such things as _____, _____, _____, etc. (Hebrews 1:1).

16. Not only is Jesus the _____ of the _____ Testament, Jesus is _____ of _____ things and _____ of _____ (Hebrews 1:2, see IN DEPTH).

17. Christ is _____ to the angels (Hebrews 1:4–9, see IN DEPTH).

18. In Hebrews 1:8, the author demonstrates the equality of Jesus with _____.

COMMITTING TO THE WORD

19. "Thou hast loved _____, and hated _____; therefore _____, even thy _____, hath _____ thee with the _____ of _____ above thy fellows" (Hebrews 1:9).

WALKING IN THE WORD

20. Discuss how you can demonstrate the correct view of who Jesus is. _____

_____

_____

_____

_____

_____

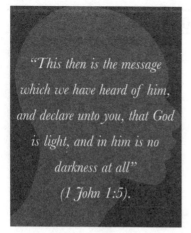

"This then is the message which we have heard of him, and declare unto you, that God is light, and in him is no darkness at all" (1 John 1:5).

LIGHT THAT CONQUERS

1   J O H N   1 : 1 — 2 : 5

Use with Bible Study Guide 3.

MORE WORDS AND PHRASES

Match the words, phrases, or names with the correct definitions.

1. _____ John

2. _____ Gnosticism

3. _____ Christ

4. _____ walking in darkness

5. _____ Incarnation

6. _____ light

7. _____ propitiation

a. a means whereby sin is covered and remitted

b. makes fellowship with God impossible

c. represents what is good

d. Christ is God in the flesh

e. taught that the spirit and body were two separate entities

f. Jesus' most intimate earthly friend

g. the eternal "Word of life"

JUMP-STARTING THE LESSON

8. In the IN FOCUS story, what "light" did Rose need to see to lift her depression?

_____

_____

_____

UNDERSTANDING THE LESSON

9. In 1 John 1:1, why is Jesus called, the "Word of life"? _____

_____

_____

10. According to 1 John 1:2-3, why is John qualified to talk

about Jesus? _____

_____

_____

11. What were three purposes for Paul writing 1 John 1:1–2:5?

a. _____

_____

b. _____

_____

c. _____

12. According to 1 John 1:1–2:5, what are two characteristics of people who "walk in darkness"?

a. _____

b. _____

13. According to 1 John 1:7, what are five characteristics of those who "walk in the light"?

a. _____ d. _____

b. _____ e. _____

c. _____

14. What does 1 John 1:1–2:5 say about "sin"?

a. _____

b._____

c. _____

d. _____

e. _____

f. _____

g. _____

15. What does 1 John 1:9 say about God's forgiveness? Why is this good news for us?

_____

_____

_____

16. If a person says that he knows the Lord, but does not keep God's commandments; he is a liar (1 John 2:4).

True   False

17. A believer is truly saved if he/she keeps God's Word (1 John 2:5).   True   False

COMMITTING TO THE WORD

18. Memorize and write 1 John 1:5. _____

_____

_____

WALKING IN THE WORD

Memorize, write, and walk in the following verses:

19. 1 John 1:7 _____

_____

_____

20. 1 John 1:9 _____

_____

_____

THE WORD BECAME FLESH

J O H N   1 : 1 – 1 8

"And the Word was made flesh, and dwelt among us, (and we beheld the glory, the glory as of the only begotten of the Father,) full of grace and truth" (John 1:14).

Use with Bible Study Guide 4.

MORE WORDS AND PHRASES

Match the words or phrases with the correct definitions.

1. _____ witness   a. sin, guilt, misery

2. _____ darkness   b. Jesus is very life itself

3. _____ the Word made flesh   c. accept

4. _____ "the Light"   d. affirm what one has experienced, know, heard, and seen

5. _____ *Logos*   e. those who have received the *Logos*

6. _____ receive   f. another name for Jesus

7. _____ children of God   g. John's description of Jesus' incarnation

JUMP-STARTING THE LESSON

8. In the IN FOCUS story, why was Paula's grandfather upset with the family?

_____

_____

9. What was her grandfather's concern? _____

_____

UNDERSTANDING THE LESSON

10. In John 1:1, what is the significance of the phrase "in the beginning"? _____

_____

_____

11. What are four key facts about Jesus presented in John 1:1–3?

a. _____

b. _____

c. _____

d. _____

12. In John 1:5, 7, and 9, Jesus is described as "the Light."

True   False

13. In John 1:6, the "John" spoken of is the apostle John.

True   False

14. John the Baptist was sent to "witness" or "testify" to the world concerning Jesus (John 1:7). What does this mean? _____

_____

_____

15. According to John 1:12, how do we become children of God?

_____

_____

16. In John 1:14, what is the significance of the phrase "dwelt among us"?

_____

_____

17. In John 1:16, what have we received because of God's grace? _____

_____

_____

18. The law came through Moses, but through Jesus came _____ and _____ (John 1:17).

COMMITTING TO THE WORD

19. Describe some of the ways God has been revealed to you through His Son, Jesus. Then, record a specific time when you gained deeper insight into God's character by reading His Word.

_____

_____

_____

_____

_____

_____

WALKING IN THE WORD

20. How would your life be different if you spent more time getting to know Jesus, the personal Word? List five specific ways you could deepen your relationship.

a. _____

b. _____

c. _____

d. _____

e. _____

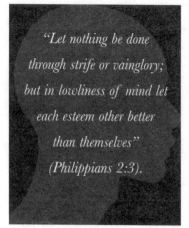

"Let nothing be done through strife or vainglory; but in lowliness of mind let each esteem other better than themselves" (Philippians 2:3).

HUMILIATION AND EXALTATION

P H I L I P P I A N S   2 : 1 – 1 1

Use with Bible Study Guide 5.

MORE WORDS AND PHRASES

Match the words or phrases with the correct definitions.

1. ____ mind of Christ

a. humbleness, meekness

2. ____ God

b. to be lifted up

3. ____ exalted

c. Yahweh

4. ____ selfish ambition

d. common disposition to work together

5. ____ name above every name

e. one of the acts of the sinful nature

6. ____ like-minded

f. having the same attitude as Jesus

7. ____ humility

g. Jesus Christ

JUMP-STARTING THE LESSON

8. In the IN FOCUS story, how was Margie's Christian walk different from Ben's?

_____

_____

_____

_____

9. What was Ben "really" concerned about when it came to Margie running and winning political office?

_____

_____

_____

UNDERSTANDING THE LESSON

10. In Philippians 2:2, what are two specific ways the Philippian Christians could bring joy to the apostle Paul?

a._____

b. _____

11. How does our standing in Christ affect our humility

(Philippians 2:3–4)?

_____

_____

12. According to Philippians 2:3–4, what does "humility" look like?

a. _____

b. _____

c. _____

13. In Philippians 2:7, what does the phrase "made himself of no reputation" mean?

_____

_____

14. Jesus displayed His humility through obedience.   True   False

15. Compare and contrast Jesus' position in Philippians 2:8–9. _____

_____

_____

16. In Philippians 2:9, what is the name given to Jesus that is "above every name"? _____

17. According to Philippians 2:10–11, what is the ultimate response of mankind to the exaltation of Jesus Christ?

_____

_____

18. According to Philippians 2:11, what is the ultimate consequence of Jesus' humiliation and exaltation?

_____

_____

COMMITTING TO THE WORD

19. Memorize and write the following verses.

Philippians 2:3: _____

_____

Philippians 2:4: _____

_____

_____

WALKING IN THE WORD

20. List three ways that you can get the mind of Christ.

a. _____

b. _____

c. _____

Then memorize, write, and walk in Philippians 2:5. _____

_____

"I AM FROM ABOVE"

JOHN 8:31–38, 48–56, 58–59

> *"Then said Jesus to those Jews which believed on him, If ye continue in my word, then are ye my disciples indeed; And ye shall know the truth, and the truth shall make you free"* (John 8:31–32).

Use with Bible Study Guide 6.

MORE WORDS AND PHRASES

Match the words or phrases with the correct definitions.

1. _____ disciple
2. _____ the truth of the Gospel is
3. _____ a servant of sin
4 _____ death
5. _____ *Sukkot*
6. _____ the true children of God
7. _____ sin

a. a transgression of God's laws

b. authentic, genuine believers

c. a Jewish harvest festival, holiday

d. God sent Jesus to pay our sin-penalty

e. one who is controlled by sin or Satan

f. believer, follower, and supporter of Jesus

g. eternal separation from God

JUMP-STARTING THE LESSON

8. In the IN FOCUS story, Houdini collapsed in frustration and failure after trying unsuccessfully to open a jail cell door that *wasn't even locked*. Explain why it is that sometimes God has forgiven us of our sins (set us free indeed—unlocked the door), but we cannot forgive ourselves.

_____

_____

_____

9. From the IN FOCUS story, explain the phrase, "Christ died for our freedom, and He has already set us free." _____

_____

_____

_____

_____

_____

_____

_____

UNDERSTANDING THE LESSON

10. In John 8:49, Jesus answered, "I have not a devil; but I honour my Father, and ye do dishonour me." How did the Jews dishonour Jesus (vv. 48, 59)? _____

_____

_____

11. Who did Jesus refer to when He said, "And I seek not mine own glory: there is one that seeketh and judgeth" (v. 50)? _____

12. Write "True" or "False" before each of the following statements. In John 8:51, the phrase "never see death" means:

_____ shall live eternally

_____ to obtain eternal life

_____ shall be raised up to life where there shall be no more physical death

13. In John 8:52, Jesus says, "If a man keep my _____, he shall _____ taste of _____."

14. The Jews asked Jesus, "Art thou greater than our father _____" (John 8:53)?

15. In John 8:54, Jesus answered, "If I honour _____, my honour is _____:
It is my _____ that honoureth _____; of whom ye say, that he is your
_____."

16. Abraham was unhappy to see the day of Jesus' coming (His day): and he did not see it, and was sad
(John 8:56).   True   False

17. Jesus said to the Jews in John 8:58, "Verily, verily, I say unto you, Before Abraham was, I am." This was
declaring His _____.

18. When Jesus said in John 8:58 that He was "I am," He was again making Himself _____ to
_____, which the Jews considered _____.

COMMITTING TO THE WORD

19. Memorize and write John 8:31–32, the KEEP IN MIND verse.

_____

_____

WALKING IN THE WORD

20. Explain what the KEEP IN MIND verse, John 8:31–32, means and how you can obey it.

_____

_____

_____

_____

_____

_____

JESUS IS AUTHORITY AND JUDGE

J O H N   5 : 1 9 – 2 9

"Verily, verily, I say unto you, He that heareth my word, and believeth on him that sent me, hath everlasting life, and shall not come into condemnation; but is passed from death unto life." (John 5:24).

Use with Bible Study Guide 7.

MORE WORDS AND PHRASES

Match the words or phrases with the correct definitions.

1. _____ authority

2. _____ eternal life

3. _____ judge

4. _____ Jesus made Himself equal with God.

5. _____ "the hour is coming"

a. end times

b. Jesus and God are One.

c. power

d. everlasting

e. evaluator

JUMP-STARTING THE LESSON

6. Give Steve (from the IN FOCUS story) three easy steps to receive salvation.

a. _____

b. _____

c. _____

UNDERSTANDING THE LESSON

7. Why was Jesus the only one who could die a substitutionary death for our sins (see THE PEOPLE, PLACES, AND TIMES)? _____

_____

8. Why did the apostle John write the gospel of John (see THE PEOPLE, PLACES, AND TIMES)?

_____

_____

9. In today's Scripture, why was Jesus in Jerusalem (see

BACKGROUND)? _____

_____

10. Why were the Jewish leaders angry because Jesus

healed the lame man (John 5:19, see IN DEPTH)?

_____

_____

_____

_____

11. Jesus can do nothing of Himself (John 5:19).   True   False

12. Who is Jesus' mentor (John 5:19)?

_____

13. Jesus would do far greater works than healing the lame man by the pool of Bethesda (John 5:20).

True   False

14. What does the statement "Jesus equated Himself with the Father" mean (John 5:21, see IN DEPTH)?

_____

_____

_____

15. To whom does God leave all judgment (John 5:22)? _____

16. What is the Good News of salvation (John 5:24, see IN DEPTH)? _____

_____

17. In John 5:25–29, what kind of prophecy did Jesus give? _____

18. Upon His second coming, what will the believers who have died do (John 5:28–29, see IN DEPTH)?

_____

_____

COMMITTING TO THE WORD

19. "Verily, verily, I say unto you, He that _____ my word, and _____ on _____ that sent me, hath _____ _____, and shall not come into _____;

but is passed from _____ unto _____" (John 5:24).

WALKING IN THE WORD

20. Share, in the space provided, why Jesus is the final authority and judge over your life.

_____

_____

_____

_____

_____

_____

JESUS IS THE BREAD OF LIFE AND LIVING WATER

JOHN 6:34-40; 7:37-39

> "And Jesus said unto them, I am the bread of life: he that cometh to me shall never hunger; and he that believeth on me shall never thirst" (John 6:35).

Use with Bible Study Guide 8.

MORE WORDS AND PHRASES

Match the words or phrases with the correct definitions.

1. _____ Bread of life

2. _____ He who believes in Jesus

3. _____ Jesus, the Son of God

4. _____ eternal life

5. _____ five barley loaves

6. _____ synagogue

7. _____ the Holy Spirit

8. _____ anyone thirsty

a. given to those who believe on Jesus

b. Jesus used them to feed 5,000

c. the place where Jesus taught in Judea

d. let him come to Jesus and drink

e. will never be thirsty.

f. empowers the believer

g. Jesus

h. came to fulfill His Father's will.

JUMP-STARTING THE LESSON

9. In the IN FOCUS story, while still struggling to rebuild their lives after Hurricane Katrina, why did Diane feel that Jesus, the Bread of Life," had forsaken her?

_____

_____

_____

10. Name two kinds of food God had already supplied for Diane and her family:

a. _____

b. _____

UNDERSTANDING THE LESSON

11. What does the Bread of Life symbolize (see THE PEOPLE, PLACES, AND TIMES)?

_____

_____

_____

_____

_____

12. According to THE PEOPLE, PLACES, AND TIMES, why did God establish the "Passover Feast" for the Israelites?

_____

_____

_____

_____

13. Jesus declared that He is the Bread of Life and that God sent Him from heaven to give _____ _____ (see BACKGROUND).

14. In John 6:35, Jesus identified Himself as the Bread of Life that satisfies _____.

15. Jesus said in John 6:39 that "this is the _____ will which hath sent me, that of all which he hath given me I should lose _____, but should raise it up again at the _____ _____."

16. "And this is the _____ of him that sent me, that _____ _____ which seeth the _____, and _____ on _____, may have _____ life: and I will _____ him up at the last day" (John 6:40).

17. The water that Jesus offers not only refreshes one's own _____, it flows out to refresh

the _____ of others (see MORE LIGHT ON THE TEXT).

18. Who is the water that Jesus offers to the believer as a gift that will quench our spiritual hunger and thirst (see

MORE LIGHT ON THE TEXT)? _____ _____ _____

COMMITTING TO THE WORD

19. Write and commit to memory John 7:38, and then explain what it means.

_____

_____

_____

Explanation: _____

_____

_____

_____

WALKING IN THE WORD

20. List five ways you can feed upon Jesus as the Bread of Life in your daily schedule.

a. _____

b. _____

c. _____

d. _____

e. _____

I AM THE LIGHT OF THE WORLD

"Then spake Jesus again unto them, saying, I am the light of the world: he that followeth me shall not walk in darkness, but shall have the light of life" (John 8:12).

J O H N   8 : 1 2 – 2 0 ;   1 2 : 4 4 – 4 6

Use with Bible Study Guide 9.

MORE WORDS AND PHRASES

Match the words or phrases with the correct definitions.

1. _____ darkness of the world   a. Christ testifying on His own behalf

2. _____ Pharisee   b. where Jesus sat down to teach the people

3. _____ valid testimony   c. a symbol of gloom, oppression, and sin

4. _____ temple courts   d. those who do not believe in Jesus

5. _____ sent by the Father   e. a hypocritical legalistic Jewish group

6. _____ those who stay in darkness   f. the Son of God

7. _____ submission to Christ   g. Christ, the Light of the world

8. _____ reflecting Christ's light   h. reflects the conduct, ways of Christ

9. _____ Christlike behavior   i. the way the believer overcomes sin

10. _____ dwells in every believer   j. exhibiting Christlike behavior

JUMP-STARTING THE LESSON

11. From the IN FOCUS story, name three things that the light of Jesus can do in our lives.

a. _____

b. _____

c. _____

UNDERSTANDING THE LESSON

12. The setting of John 8:12–20; 12:44–46 is in the temple _____

at _____. The crowd had come to celebrate the Feasts of _____ (see BACKGROUND).

13. The light of Jesus illuminates all _____ and lights the way to _____ from the _____ of sin (see IN DEPTH).

14. The Rabbinic law demands how many witnesses (see MORE LIGHT ON THE TEXT)?

a. 1   c. 3   e. 5
b. 2   d. 4

15. In John 8:19, why did the Pharisees ask Jesus "Where is thy Father?" _____

_____

16. John 12:44–46 tell us that Jesus is the Light that brightens the _____ by setting believers _____ from sin. Anyone who _____ in Jesus will no longer be a _____ to sin. He/she will live a life of _____ and receive _____ _____.

17. Jesus can bring light to a dark world plagued with sin.   True   False

18. The coming of light is a metaphor for the coming of _____ (see MAKE IT HAPPEN).

COMMITTING TO THE WORD

19. Share two areas in your life where God is working to reflect more of His light in you.

a. _____

b. _____

WALKING IN THE WORD

20. List three ways that you can reflect Christlike behavior as light to people in your family, workplace, and community.

a. _____

b. _____

c._____.

I AM THE GOOD SHEPHERD

JOHN 10:1-5, 7-18

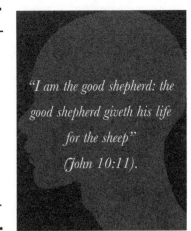

"I am the good shepherd: the good shepherd giveth his life for the sheep" *(John 10:11).*

Use with Bible Study Guide 10.

MORE WORDS AND PHRASES

Match the words or phrases with the correct definitions.

1. _____ porter

a. caves, sheds, open areas

2. _____ parable

b. brought God's messages to the people

3. _____ Pharisees

c. non-Jews

4. _____ sheepfolds

d. followers of Jesus

5. _____ other sheep

e. did not have faith in Jesus

6. _____ prophets

f. opens and shows the way

7. _____ flock

g. a story illustrating a point

JUMP-STARTING THE LESSON

8. In the IN FOCUS story, what three needs did Jesus, the Good Shepherd, provide sustenance for in Kevin's life?

a. _____

b. _____

c. _____

UNDERSTANDING THE LESSON

9. According to John 10:1-5, only the _____ has the right to enter the sheepfold and call his own sheep out to follow him.

10. In John 10:3-4, what is the significance of Jesus calling His sheep by name and leading them (see BACKGROUND)?

a. _____

_____

b. _____

_____

_____

c. _____

_____

11. List four characteristics that set the Good Shepherd apart from the thief or robber (John 10:7–14).

a. _____

_____

b. _____

_____

c. _____

_____

d. _____

_____

12. "I am the _____: by me if any _____ enter in, he _____ be

_____, and shall go in and out, and find pasture" (John 10:9).

13. What does John 10:9 mean? _____

_____

14. Jesus is the Good Shepherd not just because of His relationship with the sheep, but also because of His

relationship with _____ the _____ (John 10:15, see IN DEPTH).

15. Jesus laid down His life of His own accord (John 10:17–18).   True   False

16. Jesus took up His life again in resurrection (John 10:17–18, see IN DEPTH).   True   False

17. Jesus had authority to control His _____ and _____

(John 10:17–18, see IN DEPTH).

18. The Father in love _____ for the salvation of His people, and the Son in love freely

_____ His _____ to accomplish salvation for His people (John 10:17–18, see MORE

LIGHT ON THE TEXT).

COMMITTING TO THE WORD

19. Commit to memory, write, and explain John 10:10.

_____

_____

_____.

Explanation: _____

_____

_____

WALKING IN THE WORD

20. Share a time in your life when you knew that you were being led by the Good Shepherd.

_____

_____

_____

_____

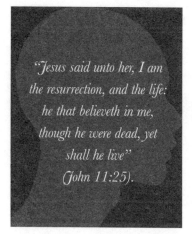

"Jesus said unto her, I am the resurrection, and the life: he that believeth in me, though he were dead, yet shall he live" (John 11:25).

I AM THE RESURREC-TION AND THE LIFE

J O H N   1 1 : 1 7 – 2 7

Use with Bible Study Guide 11.

MORE WORDS AND PHRASES

Match the words, phrases, or names with the correct definitions.

1. _____ Mary

2. _____ Bethany

3. _____ Martha

4. _____ Lazarus

5. _____ Jesus

6. _____ in Christ

7. _____ wailers

a. professionals who cried over the dead

b. holds the power of life and death in His hands

c. the younger sister of Lazarus

d. death will never triumph over the believer

e. the friend that Jesus raised from the dead

f. the elder sister of Lazarus

g. a village on the eastern slope of the Mount of Olives

JUMP-STARTING THE LESSON

8. The IN FOCUS poem reminds us that Jesus is the _____ and the

_____.

9. Name two things that the poem says Jesus' resurrection power makes possible to us.

a. _____

b. _____

UNDERSTANDING THE LESSON

10. What was the significance of Lazarus being dead four days (John 11:17, see MORE LIGHT ON THE

TEXT)? _____

_____

11. Since Lazarus, Martha, and Mary were Jesus' friends, why did He linger and not rush to help Lazarus (John 11:17–21, see IN DEPTH)?

_____

_____

_____

_____

12. When things look bad and we cannot see any way out, Jesus wants us to _____ to _____ like Martha and place _____ of our _____ in Him alone (John 11:17–21, see IN DEPTH).

13. Some scholars suggest that Martha's remarks to Jesus in John 11:21 were ones of reproach.   True   False

14. In John 11:22, Martha's faith in Jesus' ability to heal Lazarus is diminished.   True   False

15. Judging from Martha's response to Jesus in John 11:24, she is disappointed.   True   False

16. In John 11:25–27, Jesus challenged Martha to place her trust in Him as the One who holds the power of _____ and _____ in His hands.

17. Why does Jesus have the power to give life (John 11:25–27, see IN DEPTH)?

_____

_____

18. The power to initiate eternal life and resurrection through which humankind may gain entry resides in _____ alone (John 11:25, see MORE LIGHT ON THE TEXT).

COMMITTING TO THE WORD

19. Commit to memory, write, and explain John 11:25.

_____

_____

_____.

Explanation: _____

_____

_____

WALKING IN THE WORD

20. Share a time in your life when you faced tough circumstances and had to trust in God alone for your deliverance. _____

_____

_____

_____

_____

_____

"I AM THE WAY, THE TRUTH, AND THE LIFE"

"Jesus saith unto him, I am the way, and the truth, and the life: no man cometh unto the Father, but by me" (John 14:6).

Use with Bible Study Guide 12.

MORE WORDS AND PHRASES

Match the names or phrases with the correct definitions.

1. _____ Philip

a. the home of Philip, Peter, and Andrew

2. _____ Thomas

b. is the only way we have access to heaven

3. _____ Bethsaida of Galilee

c. called Didymus or the twin

4. _____ glorify the Father

d. one of the 12 disciples

5. _____ Jesus

e. to bring praise and honor to

JUMP-STARTING THE LESSON

6. Give four ways that Stacy, from the IN FOCUS story, can be a guiding light in leading her husband to Christ?

a. _____

b. _____

c. _____

d. _____

7. According to the IN FOCUS story, at some point in life, we all have been lost or needed

_____ and _____.

UNDERSTANDING THE LESSON

8. During Jesus' ministry, He repeatedly prepared the disciples for His approaching _____

and _____ (see BACKGROUND).

9. In John 14:1-14, John ushers in _____ as a comfort to relieve the anxious disciples (see MORE LIGHT ON THE TEXT).

10. When will Christ usher the children of God to our eternal home (John 14:3, see MORE LIGHT ON THE TEXT)?

_____

_____.

11. Thomas' words to Jesus in John 14:5, showed that he did not _____ what Jesus was saying to him in John 14:4.

See John 14:5–14 and IN DEPTH to answer the following.

12. You can get to God through any religion as long as you follow it sincerely.   True   False

13. There is room enough in heaven for all who believe in Jesus.   True   False

14. Jesus is the only way to the Father.   True   False

15. To ask for something in Christ's name means to end your prayer request with the words, "In Jesus' name."
True   False

16. Jesus will come, in our heavenly home, and receive us personally unto Himself.   True   False

17. Like the disciples, placing our faith in Jesus will cause us to lead lives that exhibit the _____ of God (John 14:12–14, see IN DEPTH).

18. According to John 14:13–14 and MORE LIGHT ON THE TEXT, when can we ask God for anything in Jesus' name and He will do it?

a. _____

b. _____

c. _____

d. _____

COMMITTING TO THE WORD

19. Commit to memory, write, and explain John 14:1–3.

" _____

_____

_____

_____

_____

_____

_____ ."

Explanation: _____

_____

_____

WALKING IN THE WORD

20. Share a time in your life when you trusted the Lord during a difficult situation and were overcome by His comfort. _____

_____

_____

_____

_____

_____

_____ .

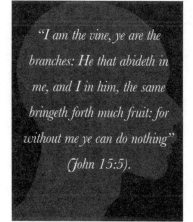

"I am the vine, ye are the branches: He that abideth in me, and I in him, the same bringeth forth much fruit: for without me ye can do nothing" (John 15:5).

I AM THE TRUE VINE

J O H N   1 5 : 1 – 1 7

Use with Bible Study Guide 13.

MORE WORDS AND PHRASES

Match the words, phrases, or names with the correct definitions.

1. _____ separating or cutting off   a. disciples

2. _____ comparison   b. remain, not depart

3. _____ abide   c. fruitfulness

4. _____ productivity   d. pruning

5. _____ followers of Jesus   e. analogy, similarity

JUMP-STARTING THE LESSON

6. In the IN FOCUS story, what can Kim do to reconnect to the "True Vine"—the One who can supply her every need?

a. _____

b. _____

c. _____

d. _____

7. Why do you think that Kim's mother's death caused her to disconnect from God in the first place?

_____

_____

UNDERSTANDING THE LESSON

8. Explain the gardening analogy found in John 15:1–2: Jesus is the _____ _____ ;

believers are the _____; and God, the

Father is the _____

_____

_____

(see BACKGROUND).

9. The branches cannot _____ or _____

unless they are connected to the _____ (see

BACKGROUND).

10. Who is the "Vinedresser" and what is His relationship to

the vineyard (see BACKGROUND)? _____

_____

11. In the body of Christ, who is the only one secure connection to God (see BACKGROUND)?

_____ _____

12. In the Old Testament, the vine was symbolic of _____ and the grapes (i.e., fruit) symbolized

_____ _____ in doing God's work on earth (John 15:1–3, see IN DEPTH).

13. The fruitful branches of John 15:1–3 are synonymous with _____ _____

who, by their living _____ with _____, are tenderly and lovingly cared for to

_____ more fruit (see IN DEPTH).

14. Three things that can cause a believer's spiritual life to become barren and unfruitful—to be disconnected from

the Vine (God) are (John 15:1–3, see IN DEPTH):

a. _____

b. _____

c. _____

15. The Master does not consider fellowship with Him a matter of great importance (John 15:4–8, see IN DEPTH).   True   False

16. Believers need to abide or remain in Jesus to stay connected to Him (John 15:4–8, see IN DEPTH).

True   False

17. The highest expression of Jesus' love for us was expressed on the _____ (John 15:9–11, see IN DEPTH).

18. To live as a branch on the vine means that one has to wholeheartedly commit to doing what three things (John 15:12–17, see IN DEPTH)?

a. _____

b. _____

c. _____

COMMITTING TO THE WORD

19. Commit to memory, write, and explain John 15:12.

" _____

_____."

Explanation:

_____

_____

_____

WALKING IN THE WORD

20. List some ways that you can bring honor to the "True Vine," Jesus Christ, during the upcoming week.

a. _____

b. _____

c. _____

THE LIGHT OF LOVE

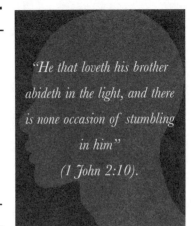

"He that loveth his brother abideth in the light, and there is none occasion of stumbling in him" (1 John 2:10).

1   J O H N   2 : 7 – 1 1 ;   1 5 – 1 7

Use with Bible Study Guide 1.

MORE WORDS AND PHRASES

Match the words, phrases, or names with the correct definitions.

1. _____ antichrists   a. code or system of beliefs

2. _____ darkness   b. Jesus, who dispels the darkness in our lives and the world

3. _____ doctrine   c. conventional, mainstream, traditional, or established

4. _____ John   d. the totality of human existence under the influence of Satan

5. _____ lust of the eyes   e. self-glorification

6. _____ lust of the flesh   f. means "gift of God"

7. _____ orthodox   g. false teachers

8. _____ pride of life   h. materialism

9. _____ the world   i. sensual indulgences

10. ____ true light   j. sin; disobeying God's Word

JUMP-STARTING THE LESSON

11. In the IN FOCUS story, the real issue between Dexter and Gordon was a lack of _____.

12. This story illustrates the importance of reconciliation and showing _____ for _____ and _____ for _____.

UNDERSTANDING THE LESSON

13. Give one reason why the apostle John wrote the first epistle (letter) of John (see

BACKGROUND). _____

14. Early Gnosticism challenged Christian doctrines involving (see BACKGROUND):

a. _____ c. _____

b. _____

15. Explain the paradox in 1 John 2:7–8, where the old commandment John writes is new (see IN DEPTH). _____

_____

_____

_____

16. Self-love is no longer the Christian standard for loving others; the _____ love of

_____ is (1 John 2:8, see MORE LIGHT ON THE TEXT).

17. Anyone who calls herself/himself a Christian but continuously hates another is, in reality, still living in

_____ (1 John 2:9, see MORE LIGHT ON THE TEXT).

18. "For all that is in the world, the lust of the _____, and the lust of the _____, and the

_____ of _____, is not of the _____, but is of the _____ "
(1 John 2:16).

COMMITTING TO THE WORD

19. Identify all the sources you draw upon to maintain and enhance your spiritual life. Reevaluate your commitment to these in light of any new insights you gained from the lesson.

_____

_____

_____

_____

_____

WALKING IN THE WORD

20. To address the gap between ideals and action that often exists in areas of our lives, what are some practical ways Christians can show love to other Christians? Identify obstacles and supports available for you to do this.

_____

_____

_____

_____

_____

_____

_____

_____

> *"Beloved, now are we the sons of God, and it doth not yet appear what we shall be: but we know that, when he shall appear, we shall be like him; for we shall see him as he is"* (1 John 3:2).

THE TEST OF LOVE

1   J O H N   3 : 1 1 – 2 4

Use with Bible Study Guide 2.

MORE WORDS AND PHRASES

Match the words or phrases with the correct definitions.

1. _____ bowels of compassion

2. _____ Jesus' atoning death

3. _____ moral murder

4. _____ righteous living

5. _____ self-righteous

6. _____ self-sacrifice

7. _____ to exalt our flesh

8. _____ to keep Jesus at the center of our lives

a. how Jesus paid our sin-penalty

b. our righteousness is rooted in Jesus

c. to give of one's self to benefit another

d. to glorify ourselves

e. to have an intimate relationship with God

f. our heart—the inner door of tender mercy

g. hatred of one's brother or sister

h. to seek the approval of man

JUMP-STARTING THE LESSON

9. In the IN FOCUS story, after the car accident, what three things did Randy realize were eating away at him? a. _____ b. _____ c. _____

10. This story illustrates that believers should resist _____ and _____ of one another, and submit to _____.

UNDERSTANDING THE LESSON

11. In chapter 3, John presents God as "_____," and out of this _____, we are given the permission to become the _____ of _____ (see BACKGROUND).

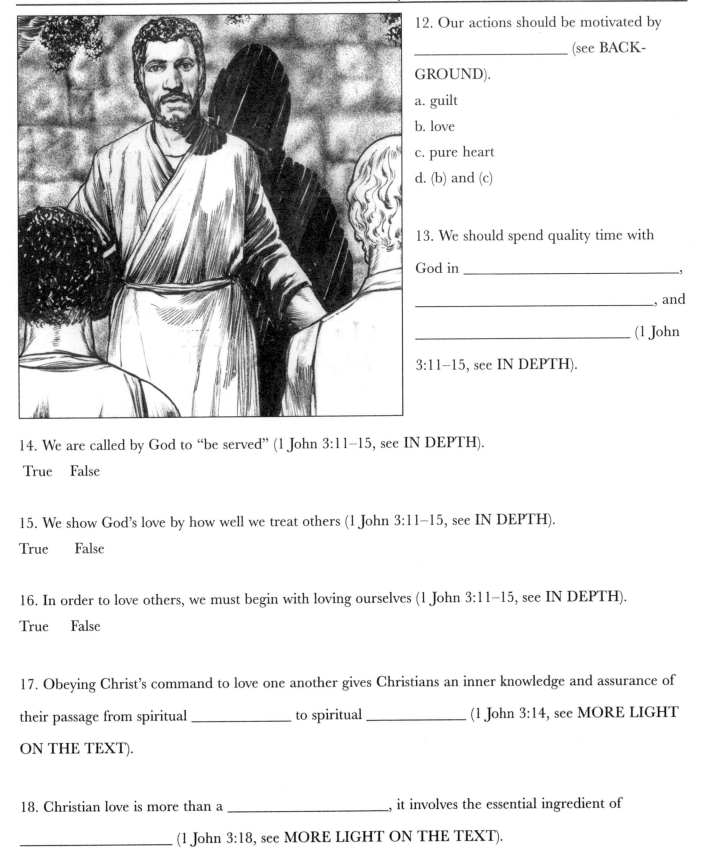

12. Our actions should be motivated by
_____ (see BACK-
GROUND).
a. guilt
b. love
c. pure heart
d. (b) and (c)

13. We should spend quality time with
God in _____,
_____, and
_____ (1 John
3:11–15, see IN DEPTH).

14. We are called by God to "be served" (1 John 3:11–15, see **IN DEPTH**).
  True   False

15. We show God's love by how well we treat others (1 John 3:11–15, see **IN DEPTH**).
True   False

16. In order to love others, we must begin with loving ourselves (1 John 3:11–15, see **IN DEPTH**).
True   False

17. Obeying Christ's command to love one another gives Christians an inner knowledge and assurance of
their passage from spiritual _____ to spiritual _____ (1 John 3:14, see **MORE LIGHT
ON THE TEXT**).

18. Christian love is more than a _____, it involves the essential ingredient of
_____ (1 John 3:18, see **MORE LIGHT ON THE TEXT**).

COMMITTING TO THE WORD

19. Commit to memory and write 1 John 3:23 verbatim. Then paraphrase and personalize it (write it in your own words).

1 John 3:23: _____

_____

_____

_____

Paraphrase:_____

_____

_____

_____

WALKING IN THE WORD

20. Share your testimony of how God helped you to love an "unlovable" or difficult person. How has this incident impacted your life?

_____

_____

_____

_____

_____

_____

_____

THE SOURCE OF LOVE

1   J O H N   4 : 7 - 2 1

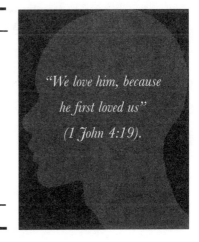

"We love him, because he first loved us"
(1 John 4:19).

Use with Bible Study Guide 3.

MORE WORDS AND PHRASES

Match the words or phrases with the correct definitions.

1. ____ Docetism

2. ____ "dwell in God"

3. ____ "God's divine love"

4. ____ "God's love is perfected in us"

5. ____ "live through God"

6. ____ "perfect love"

7. ____ permeate

8. ____ propitiation

9. ____ "the love commandment"

10. ____ "to try the spirits"

a. if we love God, we love our brother also

b. test or prove teachings by comparing them to God's Word

c. infuse, fill, saturate

d. denied that Jesus came in the flesh

e. atone or take on the sins of another

f. the full expression of God's love through us

g. have eternal life through Jesus Christ

h. God gives us His Holy Spirit

i. love that has no fear

j. agape, unconditional love

JUMP-STARTING THE LESSON

11. From the IN FOCUS story, when does God's love fill our hearts, enabling us to be victorious over any negative feelings we may have about loving someone?

_____

_____

_____

_____

UNDERSTANDING THE LESSON

12. The apostle John sent the pastoral letter to several congregations while banished on the Island of

_____ (see BACKGROUND).

13. John warns the church not to believe every

_____ (see BACKGROUND).

14. Love is just a feeling or thought (1 John 4:7–12, see IN DEPTH).   True   False

15. Love is the response we give to God because of who He is and what He has done (1 John 4:7–12, see IN DEPTH).
True   False

16. Love is a divine characteristic of God (1 John 4:7–12, see IN DEPTH).
True   False

17. At times, we fall short of God's "love" standards because of our fallen _____
_____ (1 John 4:13–16, see IN DEPTH).

18. Expressing love for one another is an outward sign that a person loves _____ (1 John 4:17–21, see MORE LIGHT ON THE TEXT).

COMMITTING TO THE WORD

19. Share your testimony of how someone extended God's love to you. How did this experience make you feel?

_____

_____

_____

_____

_____

WALKING IN THE WORD

20. List some ways you can gain a greater dependence on God's love. How can you make Him the source of your love this week?

_____

_____

_____

_____

_____

_____

_____

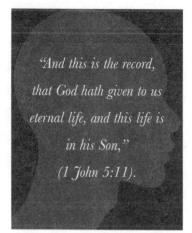

"And this is the record, that God hath given to us eternal life, and this life is in his Son," (1 John 5:11).

THE WAY OF LOVE

1 JOHN 5:1-12

Use with Bible Study Guide 4.

MORE WORDS AND PHRASES

Match the words or phrase with the correct definitions.

1. ____ agape

2. ____ "an abundant life"

3. ____ "born of God"

4. ____ "eternal life"

5. ____ faith

6. ____ Gnostics

7. ____ grievous

8. ____ "the blood"

9. ____ "the earth, Spirit, water"

10. ____ "the water"

a. everlasting life

b. an excessively heavy load or burden

c. agree as one

d. bears witness to Christ's righteousness

e. was shed for our redemption

f. saved—believing Jesus is the Christ

g. is centered in Jesus Christ

h. believed that it was impossible for deity and humanity to become one

i. evident through obedient service to God

j. God's kind of love

JUMP-STARTING THE LESSON

11. According to IN FOCUS, what is our real inward yearning?

_____

_____

12. A fulfilling and abundant life must be _____ in _____

_____ (see IN FOCUS).

UNDERSTANDING THE LESSON

13. _____ is the epitome of God's love (see THE PEOPLE, PLACES, AND TIMES).

14. Name five reasons that the apostle John wrote 1 John (see BACKGROUND).

a. _____

_____

b. _____

_____

_____

c. _____

d. _____

e. _____

15. The three tests of "true" faith that John established were (1 John 5:1–3; IN DEPTH):

a. _____

b. _____

c. _____

16. In 1 John 5, the apostle John adds _____ as another distinguishing characteristic of genuine salvation (1 John 5:1, see MORE LIGHT ON THE TEXT).

17. John states that to believe in the Son of God is to have God's testimony concerning His Son in our mind (1 John 5:10, see MORE LIGHT ON THE TEXT).   True   False

18. Eternal life is found only in _____ _____; the one who has _____ has

_____ _____ while the one who *does not* have _____ does not have

_____ _____ (1 John 5:12, see MORE LIGHT ON THE TEXT).

COMMITTING TO THE WORD

19. How has knowing your life is "eternally secured" with God affected your life? How will it change your relationship with other people?

_____

_____

_____

_____

_____

_____

_____

_____

WALKING IN THE WORD

20. List some ways you can walk as one possessing eternal life.

_____

_____

_____

_____

_____

_____

_____

_____

_____

_____

_____

CHRIST IS OUR KING

"Saying, Blessed be the King that cometh in the name of the Lord: peace in heaven, and glory in the highest"
(Luke 19:38).

R E V E L A T I O N   1 : 8 ;   L U K E   1 9 : 2 8 – 4 0

Use with Bible Study Guide 5.

MORE WORDS AND PHRASES

Match the words or phrases with the correct definitions.

1. _____ Alpha and the Omega

2. _____ blessed

3. _____ colt

4. _____ Mount of Olives

5. _____ the Pharisees

6. _____ the Triumphal Entry

a. a ridge of hills overlooking Jerusalem and separated from the city by the Kidron Valley

b. asked Jesus to rebukes His disciples

c. Jesus entering Jerusalem on a donkey

d. donkey

e. the first and the last or the beginning and the end; signifies Christ's eternality

f. supreme joy

JUMP-STARTING THE LESSON

7. According to IN FOCUS, in regard to her trip to Africa, what did Michelle need to do?

_____

_____

UNDERSTANDING THE LESSON

8. When Roman authorities began enforcing emperor worship, what happened to Christians who held that Christ was Lord and not Caesar (see BACKGROUND)?

_____

_____

9. To encourage the churches, to what four things did the apostle John direct the churches' attention in the book of Revelation (see BACKGROUND)?

a. _____

_____

b. _____

_____

c. _____

_____

d. _____

_____

10. The apostle John proclaimed a blessing upon the person who did what three things with the book of Revelation (Revelation 1:3, see IN DEPTH)?

a. _____ b. _____ c. _____

11. What was John referring to when he identified the book of Revelation as "The Revelation of Jesus Christ" (Revelation 1:8, see IN DEPTH, MORE LIGHT ON THE TEXT)?

_____

_____

12. In the book of Revelation, God divulged that at His Second Coming, Jesus would vindicate the righteous and judge the wicked (see MORE LIGHT ON THE TEXT).   True   False

13. Jesus chose to embrace His destination or mission to die on the cross (Luke 19:28, see MORE LIGHT ON THE TEXT).   True   False

14. When Jesus came to "Bethphage and Bethany, at the mount called the mount of Olives," he sent two of his disciples to find a colt (Luke 19:28, IN DEPTH, MORE LIGHT ON THE TEXT).
True   False

15. Riding on the donkey, Jesus made the statement that His kingdom was of this world (Luke 19:29, MORE LIGHT ON THE TEXT).   True   False

16. Jesus' Triumphal Entry is that of a meek and peaceful king (Luke 19:30, see MORE LIGHT ON THE TEXT).   True   False

17. Why was the Triumphal Entry important *to* and *for* the Jews (Luke 19:36, see MORE LIGHT ON THE TEXT)? _____

_____

18. What did the Pharisees in the multitude want Jesus to do (Luke 19:39, see IN DEPTH, MORE LIGHT ON THE TEXT)?
a. perform a miracle
b. preach
c. rebuke His disciples
d. feed the multitude

COMMITTING TO THE WORD

19. Make a list below of some major things God has delivered you from. Post this list in a place where you can refer to it in the midst of a crisis.

a. _____
b. _____
c. _____
d. _____
e. _____
f. _____
g. _____

WALKING IN THE WORD

20. The disciples proclaimed Jesus' sovereignty by being obedient to Him. What are some other ways you can worship God?

_____

_____

_____

"And when I saw him, I fell at his feet as dead. And he laid his right hand upon me, saying unto me, Fear not; I am the first and the last: I am he that liveth, and was dead; and, behold, I am alive for evermore, Amen; and have the keys of hell and of death" (Revelation 1:17–18).

CHRIST IS RISEN

REVELATION 1:12, 17–18; JOHN 20:11–16, 30–31

Use with Bible Study Guide 6.

MORE WORDS AND PHRASES

Match the words, phrases, or names with the correct definitions.

1. _____ gardener

2. _____ hell

3. _____ infinite

4. _____ James and John

5. _____ Mary Magdalene

6. _____ Rabboni

7. _____ right hand

8. _____ sepulcher

9. _____ sovereign

10. _____ the power of Christ's resurrection

a. to save us from our sin—give eternal life

b. a tomb

c. in control, never out of control

d. Jesus was mistaken for one

e. "sons of thunder"

f. symbolizes power and authority

g. a title that means "my great master"

h. literally means the unseen world or realm

i. seven devils had gone out of her

j. unlimited

JUMP-STARTING THE LESSON

11. According to IN FOCUS, what does Paul, in his drug addiction, need to know, appreciate, and tap into? _____

_____

UNDERSTANDING THE LESSON

12. God gave the vision in Revelation to the apostle John so that the persecuted church would know that Jesus has victory over what three things (Revelation 1:12, see MORE LIGHT ON TEXT)?

a. _____

b. _____

c. _____

13. In Revelation 1:17, where John saw a revelation of God and His glory, the word "glory" refers to what three things in the New Testament (see MORE LIGHT ON THE TEXT)? God's:

a. _____

b. _____

c. _____

14. Jesus, Himself, reveals to John who Jesus really is—His very sovereignty (Revelation 1:18, see MORE LIGHT ON THE TEXT).   True   False

15. Mary Magdalene came early to the sepulchre to complete the work of preparing the body of Jesus because she wanted to beat the other women to the tomb (John 20:11, see MORE LIGHT ON THE TEXT).
True   False

16. Upon entering the sepulchre, Mary saw three angels in white who represented the Father, Son, and Holy Spirit (John 20:12, see MORE LIGHT ON THE TEXT).   True   False

17. We have life through _____ _____ (John 20:30-31, see MORE LIGHT ON THE TEXT).

18. If we believe on the Lord Jesus Christ, we will have _____ _____ (John

20:30–31, see IN DEPTH, MORE LIGHT ON THE TEXT)?

COMMITTING TO THE WORD

19. Memorize and write John 20:31 verbatim.

_____

_____

_____

WALKING IN THE WORD

20. Paraphrase (write in your own words) and personalize John 20:31. What does this verse mean to you?

_____

_____

_____

_____

_____

_____

_____

_____

GOD IS WORTHY OF PRAISE

R E V E L A T I O N   4

"Thou art worthy, O Lord, to receive glory and honour and power: for thou hast created all things, and for thy pleasure they are and were created" (Revelation 4:11).

Use with Bible Study Guide 7.

MORE WORDS AND PHRASES

Match the words or phrases with the correct definitions.

1. _____ a storm

2. _____ occupant and permanent possessor of the throne in heaven

3. _____ opening in heaven

4. _____ the emerald rainbow

5. _____ the jasper stone

6. _____ the number seven

7. _____ the number three

8. _____ the quiet sea

9. _____ the sardine stone

10. _____ the 24 elders

a. speaks of redemption and judgment

b. indicated God's pure glory

c. represents completion and perfection

d. reminiscent of the Shepherd leading His sheep to still waters

e. a symbol of God's awesome presence and power

f. Lord, God Almighty

g. door

h. represents the church in heaven

i. represents perfection

j. symbolic of God's covenant with Noah

JUMP-STARTING THE LESSON

11. According to IN FOCUS, we should give God our _____ and _____ for what He has done for us.

UNDERSTANDING THE LESSON

12. Revelation 4 looks ahead to the _____ as the focus shifts from Earth to _____ (see BACKGROUND).

13. If heaven is God's throne and John saw a throne set in heaven, then heaven is filled with the

_____ of God (Revelation 4:2, see MORE LIGHT ON THE TEXT).

14. In Revelation 4:3, John says that He saw God the Father sitting on the throne (see MORE LIGHT ON THE TEXT).   True   False

15. The four and twenty elders represent the redeemed of the Lord (Revelation 4:4, see IN DEPTH, MORE LIGHT ON THE TEXT).   True   False

16. The crowns the elders wore were those given to the victorious (Revelation 4:4–5, see IN DEPTH, MORE LIGHT ON THE TEXT).   True   False

17. In Revelation 5, the seven Spirits refer to the _____ and _____ of God as evidenced in the work of the _____ _____ (see IN DEPTH, MORE LIGHT ON THE TEXT).

18. The four and twenty elders fell down before God and worshiped Him for what two reasons (Revelation 4:10–11, see IN DEPTH, MORE LIGHT ON THE TEXT)?

a. _____

b. _____

COMMITTING TO THE WORD

19. Memorize and write Revelation 4:11 verbatim.

_____

_____

_____

WALKING IN THE WORD

20. List some of the ways you can worship God in your lifestyle.

_____

_____

_____

_____

_____

_____

_____

_____

"And every creature which is in heaven, and on the earth, and under the earth, and such as are in the sea, and all that are in them, heard I saying, Blessing, and honour, and glory, and power, be unto him that sitteth upon the throne, and unto the Lamb for ever and ever" (Revelation 5:13).

CHRIST IS WORTHY TO REDEEM

R E V E L A T I O N   5 : 1 - 5 ,   1 1 - 1 4

Use with Bible Study Guide 8.

MORE WORDS AND PHRASES

Match the words or phrases with the correct definitions.

1. _____ breaking the seals

2. _____ Jesus' atoning sacrifice

3. _____ man's bondage

4. _____ praise

5. _____ to redeem

6. _____ the Lion of Judah

7. _____ the redemptive price

8. _____ the scroll

9. _____ the seven seals

10. _____ worthy

a. to buy back

b. the death of Christ

c. the believer's response to God's self-revelation

d. symbolize the contract is in full force

e. symbolizes voiding contract terms

f. righteous enough

g. also called the "Book of Redemption"

h. Jesus Christ

i. the ransom paid for man's deliverance from sin

j. sin

JUMP-STARTING THE LESSON

11. According to IN FOCUS, the Bible makes it clear in Romans 3:23 that "all have sinned and come short of the glory of God."   True   False

12. According to IN FOCUS, the apostle Paul says in Romans 3:10, "there are some righteous people."
True   False

UNDERSTANDING THE LESSON

13. God reveals Himself to us through what three things (see THE PEOPLE, PLACES, AND TIMES)? His:

a. _____ b. _____

c. _____

14. What question did the angel ask all creation (Revelation 5:2, see IN DEPTH, MORE LIGHT ON THE TEXT)? _____

_____

_____

15. What would have been the dire consequences of no one being able to open the seal (Revelation 5:1–5, see IN DEPTH, MORE LIGHT ON THE TEXT)?

_____

_____

_____

16. In Revelation 5:5, explain what the phrases "Lion of Judah" and "the root of David" mean in terms of Jesus (see IN DEPTH, MORE LIGHT ON THE TEXT).

"Lion of Judah" means that Jesus _____

_____

"The root of David" is a reference to the promise that God made to David that _____

_____

17. In Revelation 5:5, what does "the Lion" and in Revelation 5:13, what does "the Lamb" represent (see IN DEPTH, MORE LIGHT ON THE TEXT)?

"The Lion" represents Jesus' _____ and _____; and "the Lamb" represents Jesus' _____

18. In Revelation 5:11, what does the phrase "ten thousand times ten thousand" refers to (see IN DEPTH, MORE LIGHT ON THE TEXT)? _____

_____

COMMITTING TO THE WORD

19. Explain in your own words the significance of "the Lamb" bearing the wounds of death and why He was worthy to break the seals and read the scroll.

_____

_____

_____

_____

_____

_____

WALKING IN THE WORD

20. It is "the Lamb" of God who paid the ultimate price to take away the sins of the world. What are you doing to make sure that everyone you know is aware of His great sacrifice?

_____

_____

_____

_____

_____

_____

_____

CHRIST IS OUR PROTECTION

"These are they which came out of great tribulation, and have washed their robes, and made them white in the blood of the Lamb"
(Revelation 7:14).

R E V E L A T I O N   7 : 1 – 3 ,   9 ,   1 3 – 1 7

Use with Bible Study Guide 9.

MORE WORDS AND PHRASES

Match the words or phrases with the correct definitions.

1. ____ angels
2. ____ a seal
3. ____ elders
4. ____ God's throne
5. ____ justified
6. ____ kindred
7. ____ multitudes
8. ____ servants
9. ____ the Great Tribulation
10. ___ the perfect Lamb of God

a. to be made right with God
b. a reference to every tribe on Earth
c. people of all nations, languages, and backgrounds
d. Jesus Christ
e. a time marked by intense oppression and suffering
f. people who have been redeemed by Christ
g. messengers of God
h. a sign of ownership and authentication
i. represents God's power and authority
j. people who represent the entire church

JUMP-STARTING THE LESSON

11. According to IN FOCUS, the future of the believer is secure through the _____
of the _____.

12. In the IN FOCUS story, Vera concluded that the safest place in the world is _____
_____.

UNDERSTANDING THE LESSON

13. In Revelation 7:1, the four angels were holding back God's _____
(see IN DEPTH, MORE LIGHT ON THE TEXT).

14. There is no nation, no ethnic group, no subculture, no people group, or language that will not be represented in heaven (Revelation 7:9, see IN DEPTH, MORE LIGHT ON THE TEXT).   True   False

15. People are survivors during the Great Tribulation because they have been washed in the blood of the Lamb (Revelation 7:14, see IN DEPTH, MORE LIGHT ON THE TEXT).   True   False

16. According to Revelation 7:14–15, believers should not expect God to reward us for serving Him when He has already paid the ultimate price (see IN DEPTH, MORE LIGHT ON THE TEXT).   True   False

17. According to Revelation 7:16–17, the blood of the Lamb has secured only our future (see IN DEPTH, MORE LIGHT ON THE TEXT).   True   False

18. According to Revelation 7:16–17, the Lord Himself is preparing to meet believers' needs for

_____ (see IN DEPTH, MORE LIGHT ON THE TEXT).

COMMITTING TO THE WORD

19. Explain in your own words the significance of God securing eternal life for you and the fact that you will experience no more pain and sorrow.

_____

_____

_____

_____

_____

_____

WALKING IN THE WORD

20. How has the study of this lesson increased your commitment to rely on God for protection and comfort?

_____

_____

_____

_____

_____

_____

_____

_____

> "And I heard, as it were, the voice of a great multitude, as the sound of many waters and as the sound of mighty thunderings, saying, Hallelujah! For the Lord God omnipotent reigneth'" (Revelation 19:6).

THE FINAL BANQUET

R E V E L A T I O N   1 9 : 5 – 1 0

Use with Bible Study Guide 10.

MORE WORDS AND PHRASES

Match the words or phrases with the correct definitions.

1. _____ Babylon
2. _____ to fear the Lord
3. _____ God's infinite reign
4. _____ to honor God
5. _____ the Bride of Christ
6. _____ the Bridegroom
7. _____ the fine linen
8. _____ the marriage feast
9. _____ the marriage of the Lamb
10. ___ worship

a. the church; believers from all times

b. Jesus Christ publicly betrothing the church to Himself

c. the righteousness of saints

d. Jesus Christ

e. love for God shown in prayer, praise, and service

f. a world center for idol worship; the "great whore"

g. to revere or show reverence for the Lord

h. unlimited control over His world

i. a time of celebration and praises to God for His goodness

j. to give glory and praise

JUMP-STARTING THE LESSON

11. According to IN FOCUS, God's gift of community _____ believers.

12. According to the IN FOCUS story, when believers honor God and serve as a community with one another, we serve our _____, _____.

UNDERSTANDING THE LESSON

13. John saw, in his vision, future events that include _____ and the ultimate triumph of _____ over _____ (see BACKGROUND).

14. When believers are in harmony with one another, it ushers in a sense of community (Revelation 19:5–6, see IN DEPTH, MORE LIGHT ON THE TEXT).   True   False

15. In Revelation 19:6, the proof of God's sovereignty is the defeat of Babylon and the judgment of the righteous (see IN DEPTH, MORE LIGHT ON THE TEXT).   True   False

16. According to Revelation 19:9–10, those who are called to the marriage feast and accept the invitation will indulge in a feast composed of the promises of the Gospel (see IN DEPTH, MORE LIGHT ON THE TEXT).
True   False

17. The grant given to the "wife" (the church) to be arrayed in "fine linen" spells out the wholesome process of

_____, _____, and _____

(Revelation 19:8, see MORE LIGHT ON THE TEXT).

18. The marriage supper of the Lamb is a fulfillment of the _____ _____ Christ had with

His disciples before His _____, and it was also a _____ meal (Revelation 19:9,

see IN DEPTH, MORE LIGHT ON THE TEXT).

COMMITTING TO THE WORD

19. Share your testimony of a time in your life when you were proud to be a part of the church community.

_____

_____

_____

_____

_____

_____

WALKING IN THE WORD

20. How can your church community honor God in service to others?

_____

_____

_____

_____

_____

_____

_____

_____

M A Y   1 3 ,   2 0 0 7

OUR NEW HOME

R E V E L A T I O N   2 1 : 1 – 8

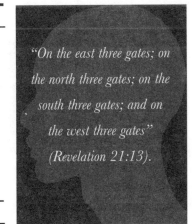

"On the east three gates; on the north three gates; on the south three gates; and on the west three gates" *(Revelation 21:13).*

Use with Bible Study Guide 11.

MORE WORDS AND PHRASES

Match the words or phrases with the correct definitions.

1. ____ absent from the body, but present with the Lord

2. ____ a fallen world system

3. ____ Emmanuel

4. ____ God's Word "endureth forever"

5. ____ millennium

6. ____ the Garden of Eden

7. ____ the New Jerusalem

8. ____ the second death

9. ____ washed with the blood of the Lamb

10. ___ water

a. accepted Jesus Christ as Lord and Saviour

b. is eternal; everlasting

c. a place where man and God were one

d. symbolizes the life that God gives to believers

e. where God dwells among His people

f. where Satan and evil powers operate

g. physically dead, but spiritually alive

h. God with us

i. one thousand years

j. damnation in the lake of fire

JUMP-STARTING THE LESSON

11. In the IN FOCUS story, how did Roger make sure that he was ready for heaven?

_____

_____

UNDERSTANDING THE LESSON

12. The New Jerusalem represents the _____ church (see THE PEOPLE, PLACES, AND TIMES).

13. After Christ dispenses His final judgment, who and what are thrown into the lake of fire (Revelation 19:20; 20:14, see BACKGROUND)?

a. the _____ b. false _____ c. _____ d. _____

e. _____ f. and the _____

14. Those that are "washed in the blood of the Lamb" have overcome Satan by faith and will have glorified bodies suited for the new world (Revelation 21:1, see IN DEPTH, MORE LIGHT ON THE TEXT). True   False

15. Christians can only experience oneness with God when we get into heaven (see IN DEPTH, MORE LIGHT ON THE TEXT).   True   False

16. Name the three types of death that the Bible speaks of (Revelation 21:4, see **MORE LIGHT ON THE TEXT**).

a. _____

b. _____

c. _____

17. God's Word and activities are fulfilled in accordance to His divine _____ (Revelation 21:6, see **MORE LIGHT ON THE TEXT**).

18. "He that _____ shall _____ _____ things, and I will be his _____ and He shall be my _____" (Revelation 21:7).

COMMITTING TO THE WORD

19. "But the _____, and _____, and the _____, and _____, and _____, and _____, and _____, and all _____, shall have their part in the lake, which burneth with fire and brimstone, which is the second death" (Revelation 21:8).

WALKING IN THE WORD

20. Evaluate your own relationship with God to make sure you're ready for heaven.

_____

_____

_____

_____

_____

_____

_____

_____

"And there shall be no night there; and they need no candle, neither light of the sun; for the Lord God giveth them light: and they shall reign for ever and ever" (Revelation 22:5).

GOD IN OUR MIDST

R E V E L A T I O N   2 1 : 9 – 1 0 ,   2 1 : 2 2 – 2 2 : 5

Use with Bible Study Guide 12.

MORE WORDS AND PHRASES

Match the words or phrases with the correct definitions.

1. ____ a vial
2. ____ defiles
3. ____ earthen vessels
4. ____ glory
5. ____ Jesus' bride
6. ____ the abomination that causes desolation
7. ____ the elect
8. ____ the temple
9. ____ the twelve trees
10. ___ the water of life

a. symbolize divine government and completeness

b. the church

c. the place where God dwells

d. symbolizes everlasting life

e. our bodies

f. a bowl

g. the supernatural splendor emanating from God

h. to render unholy, common, polluted, or unclean

i. the image of the beast

j. those whose names are written in the Lamb's Book of Life

JUMP-STARTING THE LESSON

11. In the IN FOCUS story, how did Darnell explain Sherry's death to their daughter Mykalia?

_____

_____

UNDERSTANDING THE LESSON

12. The bride pictured in Revelation 21 has not earned her status through _____ deeds.

These acts were the church's _____ response to God's _____ grace (see THE

PEOPLE, PLACES, AND TIMES).

13. In the book of Revelation, the designation "Lamb" occurs as a symbolic reference to _____ and unites the two ideas of _____ and _____ (see THE PEOPLE, PLACES, AND TIMES).

14. God will usher the church into His presence with robes of righteousness, and we will be thoroughly acceptable in God's sight (Revelation 21:9–10, see IN DEPTH).   True   False

15. The "elect" were called before the foundation of the world (Revelation 21:27, see IN DEPTH, MORE LIGHT ON THE TEXT).   True   False

16. The figurative reference to the river in Revelation 22:1 describes the _____,

_____, and _____ of the Holy Spirit in the life of the believer (see IN DEPTH,

MORE LIGHT ON THE TEXT).

17. According to Revelation 22:2, the "tree of life" bears fruit for what two reasons (see IN DEPTH,

MORE LIGHT ON THE TEXT)?

a. _____

b. _____.

18. God has prepared a wonderful and glorious future for those who put their _____ in

_____ (Revelation 22:5, see MORE LIGHT ON THE TEXT).

COMMITTING TO THE WORD
19. Commit to memory and write Revelation 22:5 verbatim.

_____

_____

_____

_____

_____

WALKING IN THE WORD
20. What are some questions that you want to ask Jesus when you see Him face-to-face?

_____

_____

_____

_____

_____

CHRIST WILL RETURN

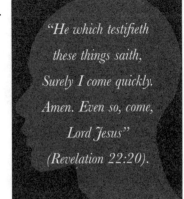

"He which testifieth these things saith, Surely I come quickly. Amen. Even so, come, Lord Jesus" (Revelation 22:20).

REVELATION 22:6–10, 12–13, 16–21

Use with Bible Study Guide 13.

MORE WORDS AND PHRASES

Match the words or phrases with the correct definitions.

1. _____ to be prepared for Christ's return

2. _____ Christ's "preeminence"

3. _____ He is the root of the offspring of David

4. _____ He was once called "the fallen star"

5. _____ logos

6. _____ recompense

7. _____ testify

8. _____ the full, free offer of Christ in the Gospel

9. _____ the time is "at hand"

10. ___ to worship any created being is to

a. eternal life; salvation

b. the entire Word of God

c. reward

d. near, nigh, or ready

e. supremacy; superiority

f. sin against God

g. Lucifer

h. to be ready; fruitful

i. to give or bear witness

j. Jesus

JUMP-STARTING THE LESSON

11. In the IN FOCUS story, why was Jason so happy that he read the book of Revelation before any other book of the Bible?

_____

_____

_____

_____

UNDERSTANDING THE LESSON

12. What was fulfilled in Jesus' first coming (see BACKGROUND)?

_____

_____

13. What will be fulfilled through Christ's second coming (see BACKGROUND)?

_____

14. It is important that each succeeding generation anticipate, prepare, watch, and be ready for Jesus' return (Revelation 22:7, see IN DEPTH, MORE LIGHT ON THE TEXT).   True   False

15. When Christ comes as King and Lord, He will "give every man according as his work shall be." This is teaching a form of salvation by works (Revelation 22:12, see IN DEPTH).   True   False

16. The book of Revelation, with all its vivid imagery and difficult symbolism, is a letter (Revelation 22:17–21, see IN DEPTH).   True   False

17. Who are the four faithful witnesses of the truth contained in the book of Revelation (Revelation 22:17–21, see IN DEPTH, MORE LIGHT ON THE TEXT)?

a. _____   b. _____

c. _____   d. _____

18. What does God say is the penalty for adding to the prophecy of Revelation or taking from it (Revelation 22:18–19, see IN DEPTH, MORE LIGHT ON THE TEXT)?

_____

_____

COMMITTING TO THE WORD

19. Paraphrase (write in your own words) Revelation 22:21.

_____

_____

_____

_____

_____

WALKING IN THE WORD

20. Upon pondering Jesus' return, are you able to say, "Come, Lord Jesus?" Why or why not?

_____

_____

_____

_____

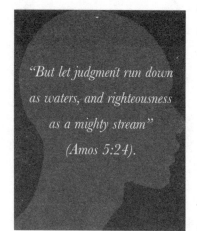

"But let judgment run down as waters, and righteousness as a mighty stream" *(Amos 5:24).*

AMOS CHALLENGES INJUSTICE

A M O S   5 : 1 0 – 1 5 ;   2 1 – 2 4

Use with Bible Study Guide 1.

MORE WORDS AND PHRASES

Match the words, phrases, or names with the correct definitions.

1. _____ Amos

2. _____ apostasy

3. _____ complacency

4. _____ hypocrite

5. _____ judgment

6. _____ justice

7. _____ prudent

8. _____ Tekoa

9. _____ "the gate"

10. ___ transgressions

a. self-satisfaction; self-righteousness

b. fairness; impartiality; righteousness

c. the place where justice was sought

d. "burdened"

e. sins

f. cautious; careful; wise

g. Amos' hometown

h. a fraud

i. rebelling or falling away from one's beliefs

j. God evaluates the motives of everyone

JUMP-STARTING THE LESSON

11. According to Tamara in the IN FOCUS story, what does God want us to do when we see injustice?

_____

_____

12. According to the IN FOCUS story, when there is injustice, God will *not* stand for:

a. _____   b. _____

UNDERSTANDING THE LESSON

13. Describe the environment in which Amos prophesied (see BACKGROUND).

_____

_____

_____

_____

_____

_____

14. In sending Amos to prophesy, God wanted the children of Israel to _____ (Amos 5:10–13, see IN DEPTH, MORE LIGHT ON THE TEXT).

15. The Scriptures clearly teach that justice is an attribute of God (Amos 5:11, see IN DEPTH, MORE LIGHT ON THE TEXT).   True   False

16. The biblical view of justice reveals that the government in a society is the source and dispenser of true freedom and liberty for all mankind (Amos 5:12, see IN DEPTH, MORE LIGHT ON THE TEXT). True   False

17. To help shape the world in which we live according to God's purpose, establishing good judgment "in the gates" can be done through our acts of engaging _____, _____, _____, and _____ evils, which are contrary to a biblical worldview (Amos 5:15, see IN DEPTH, MORE LIGHT ON THE TEXT).

18. God requires from the believer a _____ and _____ heart that seeks to totally please Him (Amos 5:21–22, see IN DEPTH, MORE LIGHT ON THE TEXT).

COMMITTING TO THE WORD

19. Paraphrase (write in your own words) Amos 5:24.

_____

_____

_____

_____

_____

WALKING IN THE WORD

20. Personally, what can you do to promote justice and equality in your own community?

_____

_____

_____

_____

_____

HOSEA PREACHES GOD'S ACCUSATION AGAINST ISRAEL

HOSEA 4:1–4; 7:1–2; 12:8–9

> "Hear the Word of the LORD, ye children of Israel: for the LORD hath a controversy with the inhabitants of the land, because there is no truth, nor mercy, nor knowledge of God in the land" (Hosea 4:1).

Use with Bible Study Guide 2.

MORE WORDS AND PHRASES

Match the words, phrases, or names with the correct definitions.

1. _____ accountability
2. _____ Baal
3. _____ controversy
4. _____ committed
5. _____ Gomer
6. _____ Hosea
7. _____ iniquity
8. _____ repentance
9. _____ spiritually adulterous to God
10. ___ the lover of our soul

a. sin; evil; wickedness

b. Jesus Christ

c. to worship idols

d. a false god

e. to turn away from sin back to a Holy God

f. dedicated; devoted; loyal

g. wholly given up to her harlotry

h. "salvation"

i. argument; disagreement

j. responsibility; liability

JUMP-STARTING THE LESSON

11. In the IN FOCUS story, although William had a personal relationship with God, what did he *not* offer in his relationship with Debra? _____

UNDERSTANDING THE LESSON

12. In the book of Hosea, Hosea's marriage to Gomer is a portrait of the relationship between faithful _____ and unfaithful _____ (see BACKGROUND).

13. Sin is always sin and God will punish it if there is no _____ (Hosea 4:2, see IN

DEPTH, MORE LIGHT ON THE TEXT).

14. What did Hosea charge Israel with (Hosea 4:1–4, see IN DEPTH, MORE LIGHT ON THE TEXT)?

_____

15. The nation of Israel was suffering from moral and spiritual decay (Hosea 4:1–4, see IN DEPTH,

MORE LIGHT ON THE TEXT).   True   False

16. God held the leaders accountable for the sins of the people because He had to blame someone (Hosea

4:1–4, see IN DEPTH, MORE LIGHT ON THE TEXT).   True   False

17. God declared judgment on the Children of Israel's _____ and _____

_____ (Hosea 7:1, see IN DEPTH, MORE LIGHT ON THE TEXT).

18. Just as the Children of Israel had to do, we, too, must commit ourselves to _____ and

_____ serve God in _____ circumstances (Hosea 12:9, see IN DEPTH, MORE

LIGHT ON THE TEXT).

COMMITTING TO THE WORD

19. "Hear the _____ of the _____, ye children of _____; for the

_____ hath a _____ with the inhabitants of the land, because there is no

_____, nor _____, nor _____ of God in the land" (Hosea 4:1).

WALKING IN THE WORD

20. Recall a time when you were unfaithful to God. What did you do to restore your intimate relationship

with Him? _____

_____

_____

_____

_____

_____

_____

_____

_____

_____

"*Learn to do well; seek judgment, relieve the oppressed, judge the father-less, plead for the widow*" (Isaiah 1:17).

ISAIAH CALLS FOR TRUE WORSHIP

ISAIAH 1:10-11, 14-20

Use with Bible Study Guide 3.

MORE WORDS AND PHRASES

Match the words, phrases, or names with the correct definitions.

1. _____ cease

2. _____ He was the perfect sacrifice.

3. _____ new moons and appointed feast

4. _____ prayers of intercession

5. _____ seek

6. _____ Sodom and Gomorrah

7. _____ "the LORD make His face shine

      upon you"

8. _____ true repentance

9. _____ true worship

10. ___ Yahweh

a. how God reads our heart

b. described God's weariness with empty rituals

c. denotes beautiful blessings from God

d. God

e. their greatest sin was idolatry

f. petition God on behalf of someone else

g. abandon

h. pursue

i. Jesus Christ

j. authentic change of heart and mind

JUMP-STARTING THE LESSON

11. In the IN FOCUS story, what did Thad discover had been missing in his worship of God?

_____

_____

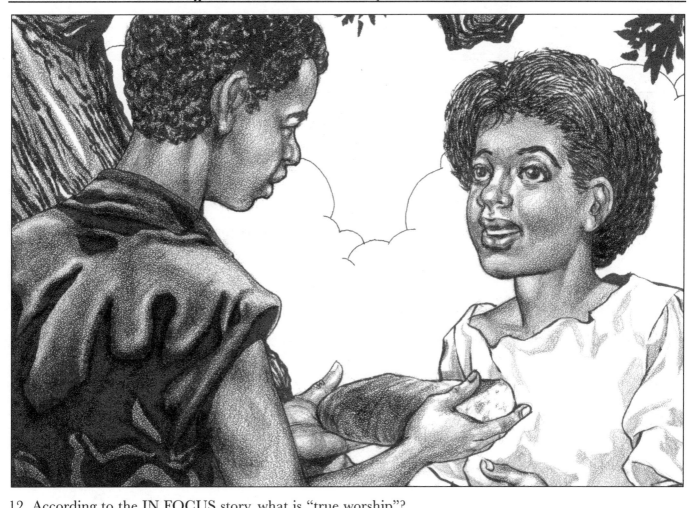

12. According to the IN FOCUS story, what is "true worship"? _____

_____

_____

_____

UNDERSTANDING THE LESSON

13. Isaiah's prophecy concerned both _____ and _____, the southern
kingdom of the once-united Israel (see BACKGROUND).

14. The Israelites' behavior and character resembled the conditions present in what two cities (Isaiah 1:10)?
_____ and _____

15. List three problems with Judah's worship through sacrifices (Isaiah 1:11, see IN DEPTH, MORE
LIGHT ON THE TEXT)?

a. _____

_____

b. _____

_____

c. _____

_____

16. Judah's sacrifices were detestable to God (Isaiah 1:14–17, see IN DEPTH, MORE LIGHT ON THE TEXT).   True   False

17. God attempted to impose His plans on the Children of Israel to force them to obey Him (Isaiah 1:18, see IN DEPTH, MORE LIGHT ON THE TEXT).   True   False

18. When we sin, God wants us to respond with _____ (Isaiah 1:10-11, 14–20, see IN DEPTH, MORE LIGHT ON THE TEXT).

COMMITTING TO THE WORD

19. "Wash you, make you _____; put away the _____ of your doings from before mine eyes; _____ to do _____; _____ to do _____; seek _____, _____ the _____, _____ the _____, _____ for the _____" (Isaiah 1:16–17).

WALKING IN THE WORD

20. Due to some tragedy that impacted your life, have you ever lost your joy in worshiping God? If so, share the experience and how God restored the joy of your salvation so that you could truly worship Him again. _____

_____

_____

_____

ISAIAH INVITES US TO GOD'S FEAST

ISAIAH 55:1–3, 6–11

"Seek ye the LORD while he may be found, call ye upon him while he is near" (Isaiah 55:6).

Use with Bible Study Guide 4.

MORE WORDS AND PHRASES

Match the words or phrases with the correct definitions.

1. ____ come to the Lord, who invites us
2. ____ God is near
3. ____ God's Feast
4. ____ God's invitation is free
5. ____ heaven
6. ____ last days
7. ____ seek
8. ____ the word of the invitation
9. ____ waters
10. ___ wine and milk

a. God's dwelling place

b. the times before Jesus' Second Coming

c. accept Jesus Christ as Lord and Saviour

d. the call to repentance

e. to investigate; inquire; to practice

f. symbolic of the eternal life offered through Jesus

g. symbolize celebration and abundance

h. God's offer of eternal life through Jesus Christ

i. God is close by offering forgiveness and mercy

j. our salvation cost us nothing, but Jesus His life

JUMP-STARTING THE LESSON

11. According to the IN FOCUS story, what two things can happen if we take pleasure in someone and do something simply to make him/her happy?

a. _____

b. _____

UNDERSTANDING THE LESSON

12. God lets us know in Isaiah 55:2 that those seeking to satisfy their soul's _____ and _____, may spend money on things that cannot _____ (see IN DEPTH, MORE LIGHT ON THE TEXT).

13. What is the "bread" that the soul longs for (Isaiah 55:2, see IN DEPTH, MORE LIGHT ON THE

TEXT)? _____

14. Our faith response should be what three things (Isaiah 55:3, see IN DEPTH, MORE LIGHT ON

THE TEXT)?

a._____

b. _____

c. _____

15. Explain Isaiah 55:6: "Seek ye the LORD while he may be found, call ye upon him while he is near."

_____

_____

_____

16. It is a duty to serve God (see IN FOCUS, IN DEPTH, MORE LIGHT ON THE TEXT).
True   False

17. We are foolish to even think or act as though we know what God is thinking or planning (Isaiah 55:8–9, see IN DEPTH, MORE LIGHT ON THE TEXT).   True   False

18. What happens when God, with His great power, speaks (Isaiah 55:8–11, see IN DEPTH, MORE LIGHT ON THE TEXT)?

_____

_____

COMMITTING TO THE WORD

19. Memorize Isaiah 55:8–9. Then paraphrase the verses (write them in your own words).

Isaiah 55:8 _____

_____

Isaiah 55:9 _____

_____

WALKING IN THE WORD

20. From your own intimate, personal relationship with God, list some ways that you have sought the Lord.

a. _____

b. _____

c. _____

d. _____

e. _____

f. _____

> "He hath showed thee, O man, what is good; and what doth the LORD require of thee, but to do justly, and to love mercy, and to walk humbly with thy God?"
>
> (Micah 6:8).

MICAH ANNOUNCES GOD'S REQUIREMENTS

M I C A H   3 : 1 — 4 ;   6 : 6 — 8

Use with Bible Study Guide 5.

MORE WORDS AND PHRASES

Match the words, phrases, or names with the correct definitions.

1. ____ apostasy   a. Judah and Israel

2. ____ compassion   b. "who is like the Lord"

3. ____ hear   c. compassion; kindness

4. ____ loving evil   d. seek

5. ____ mercy   e. the capital of Israel

6. ____ Micah   f. total desertion or departure from one's beliefs

7. ____ require   g. empathy; kindness; sympathy

8. ____ Samaria   h. "to call out for help"

9. ____ the divided kingdom   i. totally consumed with hatred

10. ___ "then shall they cry"   j. a command to listen

JUMP-STARTING THE LESSON

11. According to IN FOCUS, in most societies, leaders are held to a _____ _____ than those they serve.

12. According to IN FOCUS, leaders are expected to obey the laws of _____ and the laws of the _____.

UNDERSTANDING THE LESSON

13. Because of rampant injustice and apostasy throughout Israel, God had the prophet Micah predict what two things (see THE PEOPLE, PLACES, AND TIMES)?

a. _____

_____

_____

_____

b. _____

_____

_____

_____

_____

14. Justice denied to God's people is motivated by desires to pervert the _____ of _____ (Micah 3:2, see MORE LIGHT ON THE TEXT).

15. True worship begins with living out what three requirements (Micah 6:6–8, see IN DEPTH)?

a._____   c. _____

b. _____

16. Like in the prophet Micah's time, we can continue to ignore God and pay the _____, or _____ and do that which is _____ (Micah 6:8, see MORE LIGHT ON THE TEXT).

17. God is not pleased when leaders refuse to lead by His standards or when God's people do not stand on His Word (see IN FOCUS).   True   False

18. God is more concerned that His people exhibit justice to others than that they place numerous sacrifices on the altar (Micah 6:6–8, see MORE LIGHT ON THE TEXT). True   False

COMMITTING TO THE WORD

19. a. Memorize the KEEP IN MIND verse (Micah 6:8) and then write it verbatim.

_____

_____

_____

b. Paraphrase (write in your own words) Micah 6:8.

_____

_____

_____

WALKING IN THE WORD

20. Recall a time when you had to go back and say, "I was wrong." Explain what confession did for your

spirit. _____

_____

_____

_____

_____

_____

_____

ZEPHANIAH ANNOUNCES GOD'S JUSTICE

Z E P H A N I A H   3 : 1 – 5 ,   8 – 9

> *"Therefore wait ye upon me, saith the LORD, until the day that I rise up to the prey: for my determination is to gather the nations, that I may assemble the kingdoms, to pour upon them mine indignation, even all my fierce anger: for all the earth shall be devoured with the fire of my jealousy"* (Zephaniah 3:8).

Use with Bible Study Guide 6.

MORE WORDS AND PHRASES

Match the words, phrases, or names with the correct definitions.

1. _____ corrupt

2. _____ "draw near"

3. _____ Josiah

4. _____ Judah

5. _____ King Hezekiah

6. _____ Manasseh

7. _____ "received correction"

8. _____ to "not hear the voice"

9. _____ woe

10. ___ Zephaniah

a. the great-great grandfather of Zephaniah

b. God initiated discipline

c. "the Lord hides"

d. great pain and grief

e. to not trust God; to not draw near to Him

f. one of the two divided kingdoms of Israel

g. to destroy

h. to come closer to God

i. a wicked king of Judah

j. a good and godly king of Judah

JUMP-STARTING THE LESSON

11. According to IN FOCUS, what two questions should humanity answer before disaster hits?

a. _____

b. _____

UNDERSTANDING THE LESSON

12. The central theme of the book of Zephaniah is "the _____ of the _____" (see **THE PEOPLE, PLACES, AND TIMES**).

13. What were God's two grievances against Judah (see BACKGROUND)?

a. _____

_____

b. _____

_____

14. The people of Judah's spiritual condition were _____ before God because they were

_____ (Zephaniah 3:1–2, see IN DEPTH).

15. The strong oppressed the _____: the _____, the _____, and the

_____ (Zephaniah 3:1–2, see IN DEPTH).

16. Zephaniah exposed the behavior of which national leaders (Zephaniah 3:3–5)?

a. the princes

b. judges

c. prophets

d. priests

e. all of the above

17. The godly in the nation of Judah were encouraged to look to the Lord and to trust Him (Zephaniah 3:8–9, see IN DEPTH).　　　True　　　　　　False

18. God was willing to tolerate the Israelites' lack of repentance and the rejection of His will (Zephaniah 3:8–9, see **MORE LIGHT ON THE TEXT**).　　　True　　　　　　False

COMMITTING TO THE WORD

19. "Therefore _____ ye upon _____, saith the _____, until the day that ___ rise up to the prey: for my determination is to _____ the _____, that _____ may _____ the _____, to pour upon them mine _____, even all my fierce _____: for _____ the earth shall be _____ with the _____ of my _____" (Zephaniah 3:8).

WALKING IN THE WORD

20. Are you living each day as though it were the last day of your life? How? If not, share below what you need to do to prepare to meet Jesus Christ?

_____

_____

_____

_____

HABAKKUK ANNOUNCES THE DOOM OF THE UNRIGHTEOUS

H A B A K K U K   2 : 6 - 1 4

"For the earth shall be filled with the knowledge of the glory of the LORD, as the waters cover the sea" (Habakkuk 2:14).

Use with Bible Study Guide 7.

MORE WORDS AND PHRASES

Match the words, phrases, or names with the correct definitions.

1. ____ booties

a. "one who embraces"

2. ____ covet

b. fairness; honesty; integrity

3. ____ embrace

c. tablets of stone

4. ____ exonerate

d. spoils; treasures; riches

5. ____ God is "sovereign"

e. to make a person tremble or shake

6. ____ Habakkuk

f. empty; futile; pointless

7. ____ justice

g. to hold close

8. ____ vanity

h. to gain by unrighteous violence

9. ____ vex

i. absolve; clear; vindicate

10. ___ "write upon tables"

j. in control and never out of control

JUMP-STARTING THE LESSON

11. According to the IN FOCUS story, what is the message of hope from our Lord?

_____

_____

12. What was Habakkuk's question to God (see IN FOCUS)? _____

_____

_____

UNDERSTANDING THE LESSON

13. What is the central theme of the book of Habakkuk (see THE PEOPLE, PLACES, AND TIMES)?

_____

_____

_____

_____

14. Describe the times in which the prophet Habakkuk prophesied (see BACKGROUND).

a. _____

_____

b. _____

_____

c. _____

_____

d. _____

_____

e. _____

_____

15. What were some of the issues that Habakkuk struggled with (see BACKGROUND)?

a. _____

b. _____

c. _____

d. _____

16. How did God use the Babylonians against Judah (Habakkuk 2:6–8, see IN DEPTH)?

_____

_____

17. Habakkuk did not understand why God would use a wicked nation to punish Judah (see MORE LIGHT ON THE TEXT).   True   False

18. Paraphrase (write in your own words) Habakkuk 2:9 and Habakkuk 2:12 (see IN DEPTH, MORE LIGHT ON THE TEXT).

a. Habakkuk 2:9 _____

_____

_____

b. Habakkuk 2:12 _____

_____

_____

COMMITTING TO THE WORD

19. "For the _____ shall be _____ with the _____ of the _____ of the _____, as the _____ cover the sea" (Habakkuk 2:14).

WALKING IN THE WORD

20. Have you ever cried out to God and asked Him why He allows the righteous to suffer and the ungodly to prosper? If so, share your experience. If not, share someone else's.

_____

_____

_____

_____

_____

_____

JEREMIAH ANNOUNCES THE CONSEQUENCES OF DISOBEDIENCE

JEREMIAH 7:11-15; 2 KINGS 23:36-37

> "And now, because ye have done all these works, saith the LORD, and I spake unto you, rising up early and speaking, but ye heard not; and I called you, but ye answered not. . . . I will cast you out of my sight, as I have cast out all your brethren, even the whole seed of Ephraim" (Jeremiah 7:13, 15).

Use with Bible Study Guide 8.

MORE WORDS AND PHRASES

Match the words, phrases, or names with the correct definitions.

1. ____ a "den"   a. God is without sin and hates sin.

2. ____ Ephraim   b. the worst and most ungodly of Judah's kings

3. ____ eternal punishment   c. a cave; a hole of robbers

4. ____ God is "holy"   d. a place of rest; a city of Ephraim

5. ____ Jeremiah   e. the father of the king who refused to obey God

6. ____ King Jehoiakim   f. a sacred or holy place; a place of worship

7. ____ King Josiah   g. forever separated from a holy God

8. ____ Shiloh   h. to lean on; be confident in

9. ____ the temple   i. the northern kingdom of Israel

10. ___ trust   j. He was known as the "weeping prophet."

JUMP-STARTING THE LESSON

11. In the IN FOCUS story, what question did Calvin have about God?

_____

_____

12. In the IN FOCUS story, Carl explained to Calvin that God is love, but He is also _____.

13. In the IN FOCUS story, Carl convinced Calvin of what two things?

a. _____

b. _____

_____
_____

UNDERSTANDING THE LESSON

14. In King Jehoiakim's time, how was the prophet Jeremiah treated (see THE PEOPLE, PLACES, AND TIMES)? He was: a. _____, b. _____, c. _____, and d. _____.

15. What did Jeremiah prophesy pertaining to God's house being treated like a den of thieves (Jeremiah 7:11, see IN DEPTH, MORE LIGHT ON THE TEXT)?

_____

_____

16. What was Jeremiah's dual occupation (Jeremiah 7:11–15, see MORE LIGHT ON THE TEXT)?

a. _____ b. _____

17. Paraphrase (write in your own words) Jeremiah 7:13 (see IN DEPTH, MORE LIGHT ON THE

TEXT). _____

_____

_____

18. God punishes without reminding His people of their sins and explaining why He has to punish them (Jeremiah 7:14, see MORE LIGHT ON THE TEXT).   True   False

COMMITTING TO THE WORD

19. "And now, because ye have done _____ these works, saith the _____, and I spake unto

you, rising up _____ and _____, but ye _____ _____; and I

_____ you, but ye _____ _____. . . . I will _____ you

_____ of my sight, as I have cast out _____ your _____, even the

_____ seed of Ephraim" (Jeremiah 7:13, 15).

WALKING IN THE WORD

20. Explain why a compassionate, loving, and merciful God chooses to punish sin. What role does Jesus

Christ play in this punishment?

_____

_____

_____

_____

_____

_____

_____

"For I know the thoughts that I think toward you, saith the LORD, thoughts of peace, and not of evil, to give you an expected end" (Jeremiah 29:11).

JEREMIAH INVITES JEWS IN BABYLON TO TRUST GOD

J E R E M I A H   2 9 : 1 - 1 4

Use with Bible Study Guide 9.

MORE WORDS AND PHRASES

Match the words, phrases, or names with the correct definitions.

1. ____ accomplished

2. ____ Babel

3. ____ Babylon

4. ____ Elasah and Gemariah

5. ____ hosts

6. ____ Nebuchadnezzar

7. ____ seek

8. ____ "seek" peace

9. ____ 70 years

10. ___ "the LORD of hosts"

a. King of Babylon

b. Lord of all creation

c. to search out contentment; tranquility

d. symbolized when the Israelites' exile would end

e. to be sought; to be sought out; to be required

f. to be full; to end

g. located on the Euphrates River

h. carried the letter to the exiles

i. that which goes forth; an army; the whole creation

j. "The Gate of God"

JUMP-STARTING THE LESSON

11. According to the IN FOCUS story, what are some examples of pain?

a. _____ b. _____ c. _____ d. _____

UNDERSTANDING THE LESSON

12. Those who were carried away into captivity were the Israelites' _____ (Jeremiah 29:1–14; see MORE LIGHT ON THE TEXT).

13. List four things God told the Israelites to do to make themselves at home in Babylon (Jeremiah 29:4–7, see IN DEPTH, MORE LIGHT ON THE TEXT?

a. _____

_____

_____

_____

b. _____

_____

_____

_____

c. _____

_____

_____

d. _____

_____

14. The exiles were to trust only the _____ of _____ (Jeremiah 29:8, see MORE LIGHT ON THE TEXT).

15. How many years would the Israelites have to remain in captivity under the Babylonians (Jeremiah 29:10, see IN DEPTH, MORE LIGHT ON THE TEXT)?

a. 20　　　　　　　　b. 40　　　　　　　　c. 50　　　　　　　　d. 70

16. Paraphrase (write in your own words) Jeremiah 29:11 (see IN DEPTH, MORE LIGHT ON THE TEXT). _____

_____

_____

17. The Israelites were captured for their skills to serve the interests of Babylon (Jeremiah 29:1–14, see MORE LIGHT ON THE TEXT).   True   False

18. God promised the Israelites _____ from _____ (Jeremiah 29:14, see MORE LIGHT ON THE TEXT).

COMMITTING TO THE WORD

19. a. Memorize and write Jeremiah 29:13 verbatim.

_____

_____

b. Personalize and write Jeremiah 29:13.

_____

_____

WALKING IN THE WORD

20. Share a time when you sought the Lord with all your heart and how He responded to you.

_____

_____

_____

_____

_____

_____

LAMENTATIONS URGES HOPE IN GOD

"It is good that a man should both hope and quietly wait for the salvation of the LORD" *(Lamentations 3:26).*

LAMENTATIONS 3:25–33, 55–58

Use with Bible Study Guide 10.

MORE WORDS AND PHRASES

Match the words, phrases, or names with the correct definitions.

1. ____ "children of men"   a. God's purpose and will

2. ____ dungeon   b. abundance; greatness

3. ____ good   c. pit; well; cistern

4. ____ Lamentations   d. deliverance; rescues

5. ____ mercies   e. son; grandson; child; etc.

6. ____ multitude   f. a curved piece of wood fitted on an ox's neck

7. ____ plead   g. God chastises; punishes; rebukes; reprimands

8. ____ salvation   h. faithfulness; goodness; kindness

9. ____ "the Lord disciplines"   i. passionate expressions of grief

10. ___ yoke   j. appeal; beg; contend; entreat; implore

JUMP-STARTING THE LESSON

11. In the IN FOCUS story, where did Dexter's mom put all of her faith?

_____

12. In the IN FOCUS story, what had Dexter's mom hoped for?

_____

_____

UNDERSTANDING THE LESSON

13. According to THE PEOPLE, PLACES, AND TIMES, God called Jeremiah to:

a. _____ _____, b _____ _____, c. _____, and

d. _____.

14. Lamentations are _____ _____ of _____, which were composed by the prophet _____ during the exile (see BACKGROUND).

15. Jeremiah's sorrow was not without _____. He believed that _____ would come from the _____ of the _____ (see BACKGROUND).

16. Lamentations 3:25–27 tell us that, in times of trouble, believers should abstain from all complaining and _____ in the will of God.

17. The yoke God lays on His children is one of _____ (Lamentations 3:27, see MORE LIGHT ON THE TEXT).

18. The Lord never brings His children sorrow and grief (Lamentations 3:31, see MORE LIGHT ON THE TEXT).   True   False

COMMITTING TO THE WORD

19. a. Memorize and write Lamentations 3:26 verbatim.

_____

_____

b. Personalize and write Lamentations 3:26.

_____

_____

WALKING IN THE WORD

20. Share a time when you called on the Lord out of your pain and suffering and He heard you.

_____

_____

_____

_____

_____

_____

_____

_____

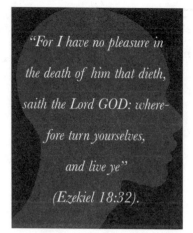

"For I have no pleasure in the death of him that dieth, saith the Lord GOD: wherefore turn yourselves, and live ye" (Ezekiel 18:32).

EZEKIEL PREACHES ABOUT INDIVIDUAL RESPONSIBILITY

EZEKIEL 18:4, 20-23, 30-32

Use with Bible Study Guide 11.

MORE WORDS AND PHRASES

Match the words, phrases, or names with the correct definitions.

1. _____ accountable

2. _____ bear

3. _____ "cast away"

4. _____ death

5. _____ Ezekiel

6. _____ iniquity

7. _____ mentioned

8. _____ righteousness

9. _____ ruin

10. ___ "true repentance"

a. eternal separation from a holy God

b. brought to remembrance; be thought of

c. involves a change of heart and mind

d. decency; godliness; goodness; honesty

e. answerable; liable; responsible

f. to lift; lift up to carry; support; sustain

g. a stumbling; a means or occasion of stumbling

h. to fling; to hurl; to throw

i. depravity; perversity; sin

j. a prophet and a priest

JUMP-STARTING THE LESSON

11. What question did the **IN FOCUS** story raise about responsibility?

_____

_____

12. According to IN FOCUS, what was the Israelite elders' complaint against God?

_____

_____

UNDERSTANDING THE LESSON

13. In the book of Ezekiel, we see just how _____ and _____ our sin is (see THE PEOPLE, PLACES, AND TIMES).

14. A key teaching throughout the book of Ezekiel is individual _____ (see THE PEOPLE, PLACES, AND TIMES).

15. Every person bears the _____ and _____ of his/her _____ sins (Ezekiel 18:4, 20, see IN DEPTH).

16. Two kings who did not follow the wicked example of their fathers were (Ezekiel 18:4, 20, see IN DEPTH):

a. David and Solomon   b. Hezekiah and Josiah   c. Jeroboam and Rehoboam

17. We can make a new heart and spirit by our own power (Ezekiel 18:30–32, see IN DEPTH).
True   False

18. The Lord pleaded with Israel to repent and save their lives (Ezekiel 18:30–32, see MORE LIGHT ON THE TEXT).   True   False

COMMITTING TO THE WORD

19. a. Memorize and write Ezekiel 18:4 verbatim.

_____

_____

b. Personalize and write Ezekiel 18:21:

_____

_____

WALKING IN THE WORD

20. Write a prayer asking God to help you obey Ezekiel 18:21.

_____

_____

_____

_____

_____

_____

_____

_____

_____

ZECHARIAH CALLS FOR A RETURN TO GOD

Z E C H A R I A H   1 : 1 – 6 ;   7 : 8 – 14

> "Therefore say thou unto them, Thus saith the LORD of hosts; Turn ye unto me, saith the LORD of hosts, and I will turn unto you, saith the LORD of hosts" (Zechariah 1:3).

Use with Bible Study Guide 12.

MORE WORDS AND PHRASES

Match the words, phrases, or names with the correct definitions.

1. _____ adamant

2. _____ hearken

3. _____ justice

4. _____ "LORD of hosts"

5. _____ obedience

6. _____ oppress

7. _____ statutes

8. _____ "true judgment"

9. _____ "true repentance"

10. ___ turn

a. conquering Warrior

b. turning away from sin

c. rulings according to truth

d. God's decrees; promises; warnings

e. to come around to the right opinion

f. hear, repent, and obey

g. determined; stubborn; unyielding

h. assent; compliance; conformity

i. fairness; honesty; integrity; righteousness

j. to take advantage of the powerless

JUMP-STARTING THE LESSON

11. In the IN FOCUS story, what was Greg's desire?

_____

_____

12. According to the IN FOCUS story, the prophet Zechariah teaches that we are called to

_____ and show _____, _____, and

_____ toward one another.

UNDERSTANDING THE LESSON

13. Zechariah called for

_____,

_____, and

_____

in _____,

_____ - _____,

and _____ (see

THE PEOPLE, PLACES, AND

TIMES).

14. What two things did God call the prophet Zechariah to do (see BACKGROUND)?

a. _____

_____

b. _____

15. Because the Israelites were ready to give up and quit, list five specific things that God called Zechariah to do to encourage them (see BACKGROUND).

a. _____

b. _____

c. _____

d. _____

e. _____

16. How many years had passed since the exiles had returned from captivity to rebuild the temple (Zechariah 1:1–6, see IN DEPTH)?

a. 5   b. 10   c. 15   d. 20

17. Zechariah let the Israelites know that half-hearted service was unacceptable to God (Zechariah 1:1–6, see IN DEPTH, MORE LIGHT ON THE TEXT).   True   False

18. Sum up God's message to the Children of Israel (Zechariah 1:1–6, 7:8–14, see IN DEPTH, MORE LIGHT ON THE TEXT).

a. _____

b. _____

c. _____

d. _____

e. _____

COMMITTING TO THE WORD

19. Memorize and write Zechariah 7:10 verbatim.

_____

_____

WALKING IN THE WORD

20. Share a time in your life when you cried out to the Lord and it seemed that He would not hear.

Looking back on that time, was there disobedience in your life?

_____

_____

_____

_____

_____

_____

> "Behold, I will send my messenger, and he shall prepare the way before me: and the Lord whom ye seek, shall suddenly come to his temple, even the messenger of the covenant, whom ye delight in: he shall come, saith the Lord of hosts. But who may abide the day of his coming? and who shall stand when he appeareth? for he is like a refiner's fire, and like fullers' sope" (Malachi 3:1-2).

MALACHI DESCRIBES GOD'S JUST JUDGMENT

MALACHI 2:17 – 3:5; 4:1

Use with Bible Study Guide 13.

MORE WORDS AND PHRASES

Match the words, phrases, or names with the correct definitions.

1. _____ angel

a. Judgment Day

2. _____ behold

b. obstinate; stiff-necked; stubborn

3. _____ "He will sit"

c. a hopeful, prophetic name for Jerusalem

4. _____ "Lord of hosts"

d. Jesus Christ

5. _____ Malachi

e. used to draw attention to an important message

6. _____ prepare

f. a military reference to God in all His might

7. _____ the "righteous Judge"

g. messenger

8. _____ the "Day of the LORD"

h. to remove and clear away all obstacles

9. _____ willful disobedience

i. a post-exile prophet to Judah

10. ___ Zion

j. refers to Jesus as Judge and Ruler

JUMP-STARTING THE LESSON

11. Forty years ago, when Pastor Long first took his pastorate, what six things did he pray for his congregation (see the IN FOCUS story).

a. _____

b. _____

c. _____

d. _____

_____

_____

e. _____

_____

_____

f. _____

_____

_____

_____

UNDERSTANDING THE LESSON

12. On what two things did the prophet Malachi confront the people (see THE PEOPLE, PLACES, AND TIMES)?

a. _____

_____

_____

b. _____

13. What three sins were the people guilty of (see THE PEOPLE, PLACES, AND TIMES)?

a. _____

b. _____

c. _____

14. When Malachi was called to prophesy, the city of Jerusalem and the temple had been rebuilt for nearly how many years (see BACKGROUND)?

a. 10   b. 30   c. 50   d. 100

15. What three things did Malachi warn the people about (see BACKGROUND)?

a. _____

b. _____

c. _____

16. The Lord had grown weary with the Children of Israel's _____

_____ _____ and _____ lifestyles (Malachi 2:17, see IN DEPTH).

17. After getting the people's attention, what four things did Malachi announce (Malachi 3:1, see MORE LIGHT ON THE TEXT)?

a. _____

b. _____

c. _____

d. _____

18. Malachi gives written notice that the Lord will surely return; He will come as Judge (Malachi 4:1, see IN DEPTH, MORE LIGHT ON THE TEXT).　　　　True　　　　False

COMMITTING TO THE WORD

19. "And I will come near to you to _____; and I will be a _____ _____ against the _____, and against the _____, and against _____ _____, and against those that _____ the hireling in his wages, the _____, and the _____, and that turn aside the _____ from his right, and _____ not me saith the Lord of _____" (Malachi 3:5).

WALKING IN THE WORD

20. Explain how you will apply Malachi 4:1 to your life.

_____

_____

_____

Answer Key

Answer Key to Lesson 1

1. c
2. d
3. a
4. e
5. b
6. The great tsunami was Jean's husband's death.
7. God sent a rainbow to appear on the pages of her Bible and reminded her of His grace.
8. False—It was *without* any action on the part of humankind.
9. Answers will vary. (a) the occurrences of the Flood and the destructive effect it had on his friends, extended family, property, valuables, and civilization; (b) witnessing the punishment of an awesome God against a disobedient people; (c) spending 371 days imprisoned in an ark; (d) starting life over again; e) wondering what God would do next; (f) wondering if there would be future generations
10. (a) covenants between God and man, (b) between man and man
11. False—God blessed Noah and his *sons*.
12. True
13. False
14. False—because blood is the *breath of life.*
15. capital, murderer
16. True
17. (a) The blood represents the life of the body. Life is God's gift to humanity; (b) the blood also looks forward to the sacrificial shedding of blood as a covering for sin. Ultimately, this was accomplished through the death of Jesus Christ.
18. God promises to remember all creation and never repeat the global effects of the flood. God emphasizes to humanity the seriousness of His pledge.
19. Answers will vary. This passage has application to such issues as procreation, family, work, productivity, wildlife, murder, the death penalty, war, law enforcement, government, the sanctity of life, and abortion.
20. Answers will vary. We can evaluate the candidates and elected officials who seek our votes by determining whether the positions they advocate and the platform of their party are consistent or contrary to the Word of God.

Answer Key to Lesson 2

1. f
2. d
3. e
4. b
5. a
6. c
7. The understood covenant was that they would love each other and cherish family life.
8. This covenant was challenged when: (a) Carmen had a series of miscarriages; (b) carrying the last fetus could cause her to bleed to death; (c) the baby could be born brain-dead; and (d) for health reasons, Carmen's doctor advised her to abort the baby.
9. False

10. God promised Abraham that He would make him "exceeding fruitful" and make nations as well as kings from his off-spring.

11. e

12. In Genesis 17:7–8, God promised: (a) that He would establish His covenant between God, Abraham, and Abraham's descendents; (b) to give Abraham and his people the land of Canaan; and (c) that God would be their God.

13. In Genesis 17:16, God promised Abraham that: (a) He would bless Sarah and give Abraham a son through her; (b) she would be a mother of nations; and (c) kings of people will come from her.

14. Sarah is mother of the Israelites and the children of faith.

15. God named him "Isaac" because when Abraham heard that Sarah would have a son, he fell on his face because he was full of joy and laughed.

16. c

17. None. However, God did promise to bless Ishmael.

18. covenant, establish, Isaac

19. Answers will vary. (a) listen to the things the Lord is saying to you; (b) trust what God says to be true; (c) cultivate a dialogue with God through Bible reading, meditation, and prayer; (d) be obedient to what you know God wants you to do.

20. Answers will vary. You can remind or share a message or a promise that God has given in His Word. If you don't know any, ask God for words of inspiration that you can share with a specific person.

Answer Key to Lesson 3

1. c
2. e
3. a
4. b
5. d

6. Minister John defined our Christian "covenant" with God as "an agreement between God and his people, in which God makes certain promises and requires certain behavior in return."

7. Minister John saw our Christian relationship with God as "merciful, graceful, and benevolent—rather than seeing God as a suspicious and vengeful ruler of the law."

8. Minister John saw that part of our covenant responsibility is to "demonstrate that we are God's people by helping others grow in Christ."

9. Israelites, covenant

10. Three things God did to redeem the Israelites were: (a) He slew the Egyptians; (b) He bore the Israelites on eagle's wings (or protected them); and (c) He brought them to Himself.

11. God required the Israelites to: (a) obey God's voice and (b) keep His covenant.

12. Being God's "peculiar treasure" was such an honor and privilege because: (a) God could have chosen any nation, but He chose the Israelites and (b) the Israelites had previously been slaves, usually the lowest people group in any society.

13. False. They were to be a kingdom of *priests*.

14. absolute, King

15. God has specific methods by which offerings were to be made and covenants ratified. Moses ensured that he followed those methods so that the covenant would be legal and binding.

16. The twelve pillars represented the twelve tribes of Israel or the entire nation of Israel.

17. Ten Commandments

18. Answers will vary.

19. Answers will vary.

20. Answers will vary.

Answer Key to Lesson 4

1. d
2. f
3. a
4. e

5. b
6. c
7. Shelia meant, "Do you want to *fly* into eternal salvation or *fry* in hell."
8. choice
9. d
10. Shechem
11. Joshua gathered the people together to make a covenant renewal with God.
12. Joshua meant to respect and revere the Lord.
13. Joshua meant to give the Lord their whole hearts and render truthful service that is both inward and outward.
14. True
15. The three reasons Joshua gave are that: (a) God is a holy God; (b) He is a jealous God; and (c) He would not forgive their transgressions or sins.
16. True
17. against yourselves
18. True
19. Answers will vary.
20. Answers will vary.

Answer Key to Lesson 5
1. e
2. f
3. i
4. g
5. c
6. b
7. a
8 . d
9. In Lena's rebellion against God, she stopped worshiping Him, left the church, and engaged in a sinful lifestyle.
10. tribal, God, deliver Israel
11. hardship, rescue, restoration, deliverance
12. The three things the Israelites did were: (a) they went whoring after other gods; (b) they bowed themselves unto them; and (c) they turned quickly out of the way that their fathers walked in by disobeying God's commandments.
13. "all the days of the judge"
14. b
15. False
16. spiritual
17. d
18. True
19. Answers will vary.
20. Answers will vary.

Answer Key to Lesson 6
1. d
2. i
3. f
4. g
5. b
6. c
7. h
8. a
9. e
10. Lawrence, against all odds, went back into the murderous Sahara Desert to rescue the lost camel boy.

11. Lawrence meant that he had to do what God had written in his heart—rescue the boy. He was writing history as a leader of his army.
12. False
13. d
14. a
15. 10,000
16. d
17. (a) Barak (a man) would not get the honor of defeating Sisera, but Deborah (a woman) would, and (b) it was a shame for a man to die in battle at the hands of a woman
18. the Lord
19. Answers will vary.
20. Answers will vary.

Answer Key to Lesson 7
1. b
2. d
3. a
4. c
5. f
6. e
7. Tamara's family interceded in prayer on her behalf.
8. True
9. (a.) prophet, (b) priest, (c) judge
10. They had worshiped false gods—Baalim and Ashtaroth.
11. (a) return unto the LORD with all their hearts; (b) put away the strange gods and Ashtaroth from among them; (c) prepare their hearts unto the LORD; (d) serve God only
12. Samuel asked the Israelites to gather there and he prayed to God for them.
13. Intercessory prayer is praying for someone else.
14. They organized an attack on the Israelites because they thought they were planning an uprising against them.
15. They asked Samuel to pray for them.
16. God heard Samuel's prayer and defeated the Philistines through confusion.
17. Ebenezer
18. False—the hand of the LORD was against the Philistines.
19. Answers will vary.
20. Answers will vary.

Answer Key to Lesson 8
1. f
2. d
3. e
4. a
5. b
6. c
7. Because Greg's parents broke their marriage vows to each other, Greg felt that he could no longer trust God.
8. True
9. Instead of the portable tabernacle, David wanted to provide a permanent home or sanctuary for the Ark of the Covenant.
10. God wanted David to rule over the Children of Israel—His chosen people.
11. d
12. False
13. The Davidic Covenant is a promise, an agreement in which God promised David a kingship that would continue on forever in Jesus Christ, the Messiah.

14. Solomon, a wise ruler, who would build the temple
15. God stated "for ever."
16. True
17. (a) David's house or line, (b) his kingdom, (c) his throne
18. a
19. Answers will vary.
20. Answers will vary.

Answer Key to Lesson 9
1. b
2. f
3. d
4. e
5. a
6. c
7. Michael prayed for her.
8. prayed, discernment, courage, prayer
9. b
10. David
11. False
12. d
13. prophetic
14. False
15. Solomon was *not* speaking chronologically because he was a grown and married man, but he was stating that in his new position as king, he was uncertain of where to begin.
16. God
17. heart, discern, good, bad
18. walk, ways, statutes, commandments, lengthen
19. Answers will vary.
20. Answers will vary.

Answer Key to Lesson 10
1. d
2. a
3. f
4. c
5. b
6. e
7. False
8. False
9. northern, seventh
10. True
11. Jezebel
12. True
13. False
14. e
15. save, restore, covenantal
16. They represented the 12 tribes of Israel.
17. consumed, sacrifice, wood, stones, dust, water
18. False
19. Answers will vary.
20. Answers will vary.

Answer Key to Lesson 11

1. f
2. e
3. a
4. b
5. c
6. d
7. He wanted to demonstrate that their spiritual lives needed constant renewal.
8. For fresh spiritual bread each day, they needed to: (a) pray, (b) study God's Word, and (c) seek God's will.
9. True
10. David
11. commands
12. Pentateuch
13. Manasseh, Amon
14. (a) the temple buildings, (b) godly worship of Yahweh (God)
15. "whom Yahweh heals"
16. True
17. a
18. nation, God
19. king, covenant, LORD, LORD, commandments, testimonies, statutes, all, heart, all, soul
20. Answers will vary.

Answer Key to Lesson 12

1. g
2. e
3. d
4. f
5. b
6. c
7. a
8. Mark cheated on his wife.
9. Mark's wrong choice cost him his family.
10. He sent messengers to warn the people of their wicked ways so they would obey His commands.
11. God used the Babylonian king to do His will—to punish His people for their sins.
12. This phrase literally means that "no healing was possible because of the peoples' refusal to repent." They hardened their hearts.
13. The exile of God's people would last for 70 years.
14. Second Chronicles gives an overview of the events that led to the exile period in Babylon while the psalmist shares the lamentations of the people who have been in Babylon for many years.
15. The phrase "songs of Zion" refers specifically to temple worship and praising the Lord in Jerusalem. With the temple destroyed and the people far away from their homeland, it was futile for them to sing songs that were reminiscent of their experience in Jerusalem.
16. False—Though the people were in exile and under intense persecution, God had promised never to forsake them. They may have felt forsaken, but God was with them even in their captivity (see Daniel 3:21–29).
17. Jerusalem was the Jews' national and spiritual homeland. There was no other place they wanted to be, especially while in captivity. As they reflected on their homeland, it gave them joy to know that despite the persecution and heartaches, one day they would return to Jerusalem. However, that joy of reflecting could not compare to the joy of actually returning home.
18. c
19. Answers will vary.

20. Answers will vary.

Answer Key to Lesson 13

1. d
2. e
3. a
4. g
5. f
6. c
7. b
8. Yes, she had forgiven herself.
9. Yes. She had done the best thing for the baby.
10. The "word of the Lord" came at the end of the 70 years of exile, where God said that He would release and restore His people.
11. Cyrus would rebuild God's house in Jerusalem.
12. kingdoms, earth, heaven
13. The "chief of the fathers of Judah and Benjamin, and the priests, and the Levites, with all them whose spirit God had raised" were responsible.
14. The people brought silver, gold, animals, and all precious things.
15. He returned to the people all the items that Nebuchadnezzer had taken from the original temple so they could be used in the new temple.
16. True—King Cyrus was a pagan.
17. They were motivated by the Spirit of God.
18. True
19. Answers will vary.
20. Answers will vary.

ANSWER KEY

Answer Key to Lesson 1

1. d
2. c
3. f
4. e
5. g
6. h
7. a
8. i
9. b
10. Albert had to make the first move toward his brother, Craig, for reconciliation to begin.
11. Answer will vary. (a) loved, (b) nurtured, (c) taught, (d) weeps
12. "Christ is Supreme" means Christ is the first, last, the beginning, and end of all things. There is none other that ranks higher than He in existence.
13. Because of a fallen world, man causes confusion, wars, pain, and more pain for others.
14. No. God has given man the freedom to make choices between right and wrong.
15. No. A sovereign God is still in control of His creation. What God has done, is doing, and will do in relation to humanity and his destiny is set according to Scripture.
16. This "fullness" of Christ is critical to God's plan; it is by Christ that God reconciled everything to Himself.
17. No, he could not. God often takes our past (what we have experienced and learned from it) and uses it for the good, to help others come to Him.
18. Answers will vary. (a) Creator, (b) Redeemer, (c) Ruler, (d) Sustainer. (See LESSON AIM.)
19. Answers will vary.
20. Answers will vary.

Answer Key to Lesson 2

1. c
2. e
3. d
4. b
5. a
6. We should celebrate Jesus because: (a) our lives are in His hands and (b) because He is the God of our salvation.
7. devotion, honor, praise
8. False
9. False
10. True
11. False
12. True
13. True
14. True
15. dreams, prophecies, rituals
16. completion, Old, heir, all, creator, all

17. superior
18. God
19. righteousness, iniquity, God, God, anointed, oil, gladness
20. Answers will vary.

Answer Key to Lesson 3
1. f
2. e
3. g
4. b
5. d
6. c
7. a
8. Rose needed to fix her relationship with God first.
9. Jesus is called, "the Word of life" because He brings life; because of Him, we who were once dead in our sins, are spiritually alive.
10. John was qualified because He had witnessed Jesus' ministry, had spoken with Him, and touched Him.
11. He wrote so that: (a) Christians may have fellowship together (1 John 1:3); (b) that their joy may be full (v. 4); and (c) that they would sin not (2:1).
12. Two characteristics are: (a) they say they have no sin (1 John 1:8) and (b) "they don't keep God's commandments" (2:4).
13. Those who "walk in the light": (a) admit that they have sin; (b) confess the sin; (c) repent of the sin; (d) turn from sin; and (e) seek to keep God's commandments by walking in obedience.
14. These verses say (a) "The blood of Jesus Christ cleanseth us from all sin" (1 John 1:7); (b) "If we say that we have no sin, we deceive ourselves" (v. 8); (c) "If we confess our sins, he is faithful and just to forgive us our sins and cleanse us from all unrighteousness" (v. 9); (d) "If we say that we have not sinned, we make him a liar and his word is not in us" (v. 10); (e) John writes so that "ye sin not" (1 John 2:1); (f) "And if any man sin, we have an advocate with the Father, Jesus Christ . . ." (v. 1); and (g) "And he is the propitiation for our sins: and not for ours only but also for the sins of the whole world" (v. 2).
15. It says, "If we confess our sins, he is faithful and just to forgive us our sins, and to cleanse us from all unrighteousness." We no longer have to deal with the burden of sin because Jesus takes it away.
16. True
17. True
18. "This then is the message which we have heard of him, and declare unto you, that God is light, and in him is no darkness at all."
19. "But if we walk in the light, as he is in the light, we have fellowship one with another, and the blood of Jesus Christ his Son cleanseth us from all sin."
20. "If we confess our sins, he is faithful and just to forgive us our sins, and to cleanse us from all unrighteousness."

Answer Key to Lesson 4
1. d
2. a
3. g
4. b
5. f
6. c
7. e
8. He was upset that his granddaughter and great-grandchildren did not attend church on Christmas.
9. Paula's grandfather was concerned about the spiritual well-being of his great-grandchildren.
10. This phrase reiterates the fact the Jesus, as the Word of God, has always been. This phrase could also emphasize the fact that with Jesus, God is doing something new. He is bringing His church into existence.
11. Answers will vary. (a) Jesus is the Word; (b) Jesus has always been; (c) Jesus is divine; and (d) Jesus, as the *logos* Word of God, is the Creator.
12. True
13. False. The John spoken of is John the Baptist.
14. John was sent to be the "forerunner." He was to spread the word about Jesus, exhorting all to believe in Jesus,

who was to come. He helped to validate Jesus' claims as the Son of God and the Promised Messiah.

15. Anyone who receives Jesus as Savior is adopted into God's spiritual family and is a child of God.

16. John's Jewish readers would have understood this phrase as a reference to the Old Testament tabernacle, where the presence of God dwelled (inhabited, resided).

17. We have received one blessing after another (NIV) or "out of God's fullness we have received multiplied grace (KJV).

18. grace, truth

19. Answers will vary.

20. Answers will vary.

Answer Key to Lesson 5

1. f
2. c
3. b
4. e
5. g
6. d
7. a
8. Margie already put her family and others' interest first and wanted to do so in the political arena as well.
9. Ben really thought that Margie's political endeavors would cause him and their children to be neglected.
10. They could bring joy by being: (a) "likeminded," i.e., living in unity with one another and (b) loving each other deeply.
11. Since we know who we are and what we have through Christ, we are secure in Him. We are then free to serve others in love.
12. Humility is demonstrated by: (a) putting others ahead of ourselves; (b) rejecting pride and selfishness; and (c) not thinking too highly of oneself
13. It means that Jesus emptied himself of all rights and privileges that would be implicit in His deity, and instead took on the humble form of a human.
14. True
15. In Philippians 2:8, we see Jesus at the lowest point of His earthly life executed in the most degrading method ever, even viewed as being cursed of God. In verse 9, God has highly exalted Jesus to His rightful place of divine authority.
16. Lord
17. Ultimately, every person ever created will bow his or her knee to Jesus and will confess His Lordship.
18. It is that mankind is redeemed and God is glorified.
19. Philippians 2:3: "Let nothing be done through strife or vainglory; but in lowliness of mind let each esteem other better than themselves." Philippians 2:4: "Look not every man on his own things, but every man also on the things of others."
20. Answers will vary. Philippians 2:5: "Let this mind be in you, which was also in Christ Jesus."

Answer Key to Lesson 6

1. f
2. d
3. e
4. g
5. c
6. b
7. a
8. Answers will vary, but two possible answers are: (a) that many do not fully appreciate what it means to be forgiven of their sins by a Holy God, and (b) many cannot forgive themselves for disobeying God's rules of conduct.
9. Because we believe on the Lord Jesus Christ as our personal Saviour, sin no longer has control over us. We have been set free from the consequences of our sins.
10. The Jews dishonored Jesus by saying that He had a demon (v. 48) and by trying to stone Him (v. 59).
11. Jesus refers to His Father.
12. True, True, True
13. saying, never, death
14. Abraham

15. myself, nothing, Father, me, God
16. False
17. preexistence
18. equal, God, blasphemous
19. "Then said Jesus to those Jews which believed on him, If ye continue in my word, then are ye my disciples indeed; And ye shall know the truth, and the truth shall make you free" (John 8:31–32).
20. Answers will vary. A possible answer to the first part of the question is: In John 8:31–32, Jesus tells true believers that if they are truly His disciples, the will obey His teachings. Jesus, Himself, is the One who is the truth that sets us free from the control and consequences of sin. He restores our relationship with God. He is the only way back to a Holy God.

Answer Key to Lesson 7
1. c
2. d
3. e
4. b
5. a
6. (a) Steve, ask God to forgive you of your sins; (b) believe that Jesus is the Son of God and He came to die for your sins; and (c) call on God to save you.
7. Because only Jesus was and is without sin.
8. He wrote to prove conclusively that Jesus is indeed the Messiah, the Son of God.
9. He was there for one of the Jewish "holy" days.
10. They were angry because Jesus was eclipsing their popularity and gaining followers.
11. True
12. God the Father
13. True
14. It meant that Jesus and the Father are one. Jesus was equal with the Father.
15. He leaves all judgment to the Son.
16. If we believe on the Lord Jesus Christ, we will be saved.
17. He gave "End-Time" Prophecy.
18. They will rise to meet Jesus.
19. heareth, believeth, him, everlasting life, condemnation, death, life
20. Answers will vary.

Answer Key to Lesson 8
1. g
2. e
3. h
4. a
5. b
6. c
7. f
8. d
9. Diane felt that way because she saw others prospering and they were still suffering.
10. (a) God had supplied physical food and (b) spiritual nourishment for them to keep going.
11. The "Bread of Life" symbolizes the manna God provided for the Israelites during their wilderness experience.
12. The Passover Feast was established to commemorate the historical deliverance of the children of Israel from Egypt.
13. eternal life
14. forever
15. Father's, nothing, last day
16. will, every one, Son, believeth, him, everlasting, raise
17. soul, lives
18. The water is the Holy Spirit.
19. "He that believeth on me, as the scripture hath said, out of his belly shall flow rivers of living water" (John 7:38).

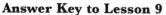

The term "living water" indicates eternal life. Here Jesus uses this term to refer to the Holy Spirit. When we accept the gift of God's Holy Spirit, He will bring us eternal life.

20. Answers will vary.

Answer Key to Lesson 9

1. c
2. e
3. a
4. b
5. f
6. d
7. i
8. j
9. h
10. g
11. The light of Jesus in our lives can: (a) overcome the darkness of sin; (b) heal better than any surgical laser beam; and (c) is a solution available for believers to overcome any trouble in our lives.
12. courtyard, Jerusalem, Tabernacles
13. sin, freedom, darkness
14. b
15. They were attempting to discredit Jesus.
16. darkness, free, believes, slave, righteousness, eternal life
17. True
18. salvation
19. Answers will vary.
20. Answers will vary.

Answer Key to Lesson 10

1. f
2. g
3. e
4. a
5. c
6. b
7. d
8. Jesus, the Good Shepherd, provided sustenance for Kevin's need to: (a) confess his sins; (b) to ask God and the choir members for forgiveness; and (c) to be made whole.
9. shepherd
10. Jesus calling His sheep by name and leading them mean: (a) the Shepherd is on intimate terms with His sheep; (b) the Shepherd knew His sheep's names and personalities; and (c) He invested great amounts of time in the sheep.
11. Four characteristics are: (a) He approaches directly—He enters at the gate; (b) He has God's authority—the gate-keeper allows Him to enter; (c) He meets real needs—the sheep recognize His voice and follow Him; and (d) He has sacrificial love—He is willing to lay down His life for the sheep.
12. door, man, shall, saved
13. John 10:9 means that Jesus is the only way and method by which sinful humanity can be saved or reconciled to a Holy God.
14. God, Father
15. True
16. True
17. death, resurrection
18. arranged, gave, all
19. "The thief cometh not, but for to steal, and to kill, and to destroy: I am come that they might have life, and that they might have it more abundantly" (John 10:10). The thief is Satan, and he comes to steal, kill, and destroy God's sheep (believers). However, Jesus has come to save us.

20. Answers will vary.

Answer Key to Lesson 11

1. c
2. g
3. f
4. e
5. b
6. d
7. a
8. Resurrection, Life
9. Jesus' resurrection power makes possible to us: (a) power to be saved and (b) power to live a holy life.
10. In biblical times, the Jews believed that the spirit hovered over the body for three days and may re-enter the deceased. Therefore, if Lazarus were brought back from death after four days, it would have been clear to everyone that a real miracle had taken place.
11. In order to demonstrate His power, Jesus waited until all hope in human effort was exhausted.
12. run, Him, all, trust
13. True
14. False
15. True
16. life, death
17. Jesus has the power to give life because He is life itself.
18. Jesus
19. "Jesus said unto her, I am the resurrection, and the life: he that believeth in me, though he were dead, yet shall he live" (John 11:25). This verse means that Jesus holds the keys to eternal life in His hands. We, being a part of sinful humanity, are dead in trespasses and sins; but we can have eternal life by accepting Jesus Christ as our Lord and Saviour.
20. Answers will vary.

Answer Key to Lesson 12

1. d
2. c
3. a
4. e
5. b
6. Stacy can be a guiding light by: (a) voicing her concerns about Derek's spiritual life or lack there of to him; (b) praying for him;(c) believing God; and (d) showing Derek love.
7. direction, guidance
8. suffering, death
9. faith
10. Christ will usher the children of God to our eternal home at His second coming.
11. understand
12. False
13. True
14. True
15. False
16. True
17. power
18. We can ask God for anything in Jesus' name and He will do it, (a) when our hearts are surrendered to God; (b) when we are living in and for God; (c) when our will is attuned to God's will; and (d) when our prayers are for His purposes, in His name, and for God's glory.
19. "Let not your heart be troubled: ye believe in God, believe also in me. In my Father's house are many mansions: if it were not so, I would have told you. I go to prepare a place for you. And if I go and prepare a place for you, I will come again, and receive you unto myself; that where I am, there ye may be also." These verses mean that anyone who believes in Jesus Christ as his/her personal Lord and Saviour is guaranteed eternal life—living for-

ever and ever with Jesus.
20. Answers will vary.

Answer Key to Lesson 13
1. d
2. e
3. b.
4. c
5. a
6. Answers may vary. (a) Kim can seek God's comfort and help through prayer; (b) She can reflect on how good God has been to her in the past; (c) She can continue to study God's Word and ask God to minister to her through it and His Holy Spirit; and (d) She can ask others to help her pray her way through the disconnect.
7. Sometimes pain and suffering cause us to blame God for our dilemma and, therefore, we disconnect from Him.
8. True Vine (trunk), branches, husbandman (farmer or gardener) who takes care of the branches (believers)
9. live, produce, vine
10. God the Father is the Vinedresser and He owns the vineyard.
11. Jesus Christ
12. Israel, Israel's, fruitfulness
13. true believers, union, Christ, produce
14. Three things that can cause a believer's spiritual life to become barren and unfruitful are: (a) not studying God's Word; (b) not witnessing; or (c) an undeveloped prayer life.
15. False
16. True
17. Cross
18. To live as a branch on the vine means that one has to wholeheartedly commit to: (a) obeying God's commandments, (b) bearing fruit, and (c) spreading the Gospel.
19. "This is my commandment, That ye love one another, as I have loved you" (John 15:12). This Scripture means that staying connected to the vine (God) will produce in us the fruit of agape or unconditional love for our fellow man. Jesus is our greatest example of love in that He loved us so much that He laid down His life for us and took it up again.
20. Answers will vary.

ANSWER KEY

Answer Key to Lesson 1

1. g
2. j
3. a.
4. f.
5. h
6. i
7. c
8. e
9. d
10. b
11. love
12. love, God, love, others
13. Because false teaching had infiltrated throughout the Asia Minor churches, John wrote to strengthen the faith and fellowship of these struggling communities.
14. (a) Christ, (b) salvation, (c) sin
15. The commandment instructing believers to love one another was old and familiar to John's audience because it is deeply rooted in Christian tradition (Leviticus 19:18), and it's new because it took on new meaning after the coming of Christ (Matthew 22:36–40; John 4:19–21).
16. sacrificial, Christ
17. darkness
18. flesh, eyes, pride, life, Father, world
19. Answers will vary.
20. Answers will vary.

Answer Key to Lesson 2

1. f
2. a
3. g
4. b
5. h
6. c
7. d
8. e
9. anger, self-hatred, guilt
10. hatred, mistreatment, love
11. love, love, children, God
12. d
13. prayer, worship, devotion
14. False
15. True
16. False
17. death, life
18. feeling, giving
19. "And this is his commandment, That we should believe on the name of his Son, Jesus Christ, and love one another, as he gave us commandment." *The personal paraphrase could be:* This is God's command or mandate to me, That

I should believe on the name of God's Son, Jesus Christ, and I also should love my fellowman, as He has commanded me.
20. Answers will vary.

Answer Key to Lesson 3
1. d
2. h
3. j
4. f
5. g
6. i
7. c
8. e
9. a
10. b
11. When we allow the love of Jesus Christ to permeate our life and become our source, God's love will fill our hearts, thus enabling us to be victorious over any negative feelings we may have toward someone.
12. Patmos
13. spirit
14. False
15. True
16. True
17. human nature
18. God
19. Answers will vary.
20. Answers will vary.

Answer Key to Lesson 4
1. j
2. g
3. f
4. a
5. i
6. h
7. b
8. e
9. c
10. d
11. Our inward yearning is actually to be in concert (right relationship—harmony) with God.
12. centered, Jesus Christ.
13. Jesus
14. The apostle John wrote 1 John to: (a) help believers realize the certainty of God in our lives through faith in Christ Jesus; (b) describe the conditions of fellowship with God made possible through the blood of His Son; (c) explain that obedience is the key to our fellowship and we should attempt to live sinless lives; (d) define how confession leads to forgiveness and allows believers to celebrate our fellowship with God; and (e) summarize the key factors regarding achieving a right relationship with God.
15. The three tests of true faith that John established were: (a) believe in Jesus as the Son of God; (b) show love for God and His children; and (c) obey God's commandments.
16. faith
17. False
18. Jesus Christ, Christ, eternal life, Christ, eternal life
19. Answers will vary.
20. Answers will vary.

Answer Key to Lesson 5
1. e
2. f
3. d
4. a.

5. b
6. c
7. Michelle needed to yield to God's guidance and His Lordship over her life.
8. The Christians were persecuted.
9. The apostle John directed the churches' attention to the fact that: (a) they will have victory through Christ in the future; (b) the final showdown between God and Satan is imminent; (c) Satan will increase his opposition against them, but they must keep their eyes on God's promise to vindicate them when Jesus returns; and (d) God is the sovereign ruler over all human history.
10. John proclaims a blessing upon the person who: (a) reads Revelation, (b) hears it, and (c) takes it to heart.
11. It could mean that John discloses information given to him from Jesus Christ, or that it unveils information about Jesus Christ, or both.
12. True
13. True
14. True
15. False
16. True
17. The Triumphal Entry was important to and for the Jews because it was Jesus' final and official offer of Himself to them as their Messiah-King.
18. c
19. Answers will vary.
20. Answers will vary.

Answer Key to Lesson 6

1. d
2. h
3. j
4. e
5. i
6. g
7. f
8. b
9. c
10. a
11. Paul needs to know and appreciate the power of Christ's resurrection and tap into it.
12. (a) sin, (b) death, and (c) Satan
13. "Glory" means God's: (a) heaviness, (b) awesomeness, or (c) intrinsic worth.
14. True
15. False
16. False
17. Jesus' name
18. eternal life
19. "But these are written, that ye might believe that Jesus is the Christ, the Son of God; and that believing ye might have life through His name" (John 20:31).
20. Answers will vary.

Answer Key to Lesson 7

1. e
2. f
3. g
4. j
5. b
6. c
7. i
8. d
9. a
10. h
11. praise, honor
12. future, heaven
13. presence

14. False
15. True
16. True
17. perfections, fullness, Holy Spirit
18. (a) all things were created by Him, (b) all things were created for His pleasure
19. "Thou art worthy, O Lord, to receive glory and honour and power: for thou hast created all things, and for thy pleasure they are and were created" (Revelation 4:11).
20. Answers will vary.

Answer Key to Lesson 8

1. e
2. i
3. j
4. c
5. a
6. h
7. b
8. g
9. d
10. f
11. True
12. False
13. Word, works, Son
14. The angel asked, "Who is worthy to open the book, and to loose the seals thereof?"
15. The dire consequences would have been that God's kingdom would never come to earth and humanity is lost in sin and has no hope.
16. "The Lion of Judah" means that Jesus is a descendant of the tribe of Judah and will return to earth as a conquering lion after the great tribulation; "The root of David" is a reference to the promise God made to David that one of David's descendants would occupy the throne forever (2 Samuel and Luke 1:31–33).
17. "the lion" represents Jesus' power and authority; and "the Lamb" represents His submission to God's will and His sacrifice for the sins of all mankind
18. The phrase means "a number that cannot be counted."
19. Answers may vary, but should include the fact that Jesus was the only one who was 100% God/100% man and righteous enough to pay man's sin-penalty. Since He paid the penalty, He was the only one worthy to open God's books.
20. Answers will vary.

Answer Key to Lesson 9

1. g
2. h
3. j
4. i
5. a
6. b
7. c
8. f
9. e
10. d
11. blood, Lamb
12. in Christ
13. judgment
14. True
15. True
16. False
17. False
18. eternity
19. Answers will vary.
20. Answers will vary.

Answer Key to Lesson 10
1. f
2. g
3. h
4. j
5. a
6. d
7. c
8. i
9. b
10. e
11. strengthens
12. Bridegroom, Jesus
13. judgment, God, evil
14. True
15. False
16. True
17. atonement, justification, sanctification
18. Last Supper, crucifixion, Passover
19. Answers will vary.
20. Answers will vary.

Answer Key to Lesson 11
1. g
2. f
3. h
4. b
5. i
6. c
7. e
8. j
9. a
10. d
11. Roger rededicated his life to Christ.
12. glorified
13. (a) antichrist, (b) prophet, (c) Satan, (d) Death, (e) Hades (hell), (f) wicked
14. True
15. False
16. spiritual, physical, eternal
17. purpose
18. overcometh, inherit, all, God, son
19. fearful, unbelieving, abominable, murderers, whoremongers, sorcerers, idolaters, liars
20. Answers will vary.

Answer Key to Lesson 12
1. f
2. h
3. e
4. g
5. b
6. i
7. j
8. c
9. a
10. d
11. Darnell explained that Sherry had gone to live with God forever.
12. righteous, obedient, saving
13. Christ, redemption, kingship
14. True

15. True
16. outpouring, deposit, flow, believer
17. (a) to confer immortality on its eater; and (b) for the maintenance of life in the Holy City
18. trust, Him
19. "And there shall be no night there; and they need no candle, neither light of the sun; for the Lord God giveth them light: and they shall reign for ever and ever."
20. Answers will vary.

Answer Key to Lesson 13
1. h
2. e
3. j
4. g
5. b
6. c
7. i
8. a
9. d
10. f
11. Since no one told Jason where to start, he was glad to know that God and believers would win in the end.
12. The prophecies of the Old Testament have been fulfilled in Christ's First Coming.
13. The prophecy of Revelation will be fulfilled through Christ's Second Coming.
14. True
15. False
16. True
17. (a) the angel, (b) John, (c) the Holy Spirit, (d) Jesus
18. For adding to the prophecy, God will add unto him/her the plagues that are written in Revelation, and for taking away from the words of the book of this prophecy, God will take away his/her part out of the book of life.
19. Answers will vary.
20. Answers will vary.

ANSWER KEY

JUNE–AUGUST 2007

Answer Key to Lesson 1
1. d
2. i
3. a
4. h
5. j
6. b
7. f
8. g
9. c
10. e
11. Tamara said that "When we see something that is unfair, God wants us to take action."
12. (a) injustice, (b) complacency
13. Selfishness, materialism, and sin were rampant at the expense of the poor, and God was not pleased.
14. repent
15. True
16. False
17. social, economic, spiritual, and cultural
18. broken, contrite
19. Answers will vary.
20. Answers will vary.

Answer Key to Lesson 2
1. j
2. d
3. i
4. f
5. g
6. h
7. a
8. e
9. c
10. b
11. faithfulness
12. God, Israel
13. repentance
14. disobedience
15. True
16. False
17. attitude, behavior
18. obey, faithfully, all
19. word, LORD, Israel, LORD, controversy, truth, mercy, knowledge, God
20. Answers will vary.

Answer Key to Lesson 3

1. g
2. i
3. b
4. f
5. h
6. e
7. c
8. j
9. a
10. d
11. He discovered that he had never entered into worship genuinely adoring God for being God.
12. "True worship" is not what we do, but how God reads our heart.
13. Judah, Jerusalem
14. Sodom, Gomorrah
15. (a) Their worship meant nothing—served *no* purpose; (b) Their worship *added nothing*—God said He had enough; (c) Their worship *did nothing*—God did not delight in it.
16. True
17. False
18. repentance
19. clean, evil, cease, evil, Learn, well, judgment, relieve, oppressed, judge, fatherless, plead, widow
20. Answers will vary.

Answer Key to Lesson 4

1. c
2. i
3. h
4. j
5. a
6. b
7. e
8. d
9. f
10. g
11. (a) We receive joy; (b) We receive the glory.
12. thirst, hunger, satisfy
13. The bread that the soul longs for is a personal relationship with the living God.
14. (a) repent of our sins, (b) turn from our sins, and (c) come to the Lord, who invites us
15. God wants us to intensively crave or desire Him, enquire after Him right now while we can find Him. He wants us to accept Jesus as our Lord and Saviour.
16. False
17. True
18. Those who are truly God's people are drawn to Him.
19. Answers will vary.
20. Answers will vary.

Answer Key to Lesson 5

1. f
2. g
3. j
4. i
5. c
6. b
7. d
8. e
9. a
10. h
11. higher standard
12. God, land

13. (a) the fall of its capital, Samaria, (b) Judah's coming destruction
14. character, God
15. (a) acting justly, (b) being merciful, (c) walking humbly with God
16. price, repent, good
17. True
18. True
19. (a) "He hath showed thee, O man, what is good; and what doth the LORD require of thee, but to do justly, and to love mercy, and to walk humbly with thy God?" (Micah 6:8); (b) Answers will vary.
20. Answers will vary.

Answer Key to Lesson 6
1. g
2. h
3. j
4. f
5. a
6. i
7. b
8. e
9. d
10. c
11. (a) "What is my relationship with God?" and (b) "Am I prepared for Judgment Day?"
12. day, Lord
13. (a) Judah failed to observe the commandments God had given them and (b) they broke their covenant with God
14. filthy, rebellious
15. weak, poor, orphans, widows.
16. e
17. True
18. False
19. wait, me, LORD, I, gather, nations, I, assemble, kingdoms, indignation, anger, all, devoured, fire, jealousy
20. Answers will vary.

Answer Key to Lesson 7
1. d
2. h
3. g
4. i
5. j
6. a
7. b
8. f
9. e
10. c
11. The message of hope from our Lord is "no matter what the hardship, no good thing ever dies."
12. Habakkuk wanted to know why evil prevails.
13. The central theme of the book of Habakkuk is faith in the midst of problems, or "the just shall live by his faith."
14. (a) There was no justice in the land; (b) Violence and wickedness proceeded without resistance; (c) Trouble was everywhere; (d) Contention and strife were out of control; and (e) King Nebuchadnezzar of Babylonia was on a conquering campaign against the Children of Israel.
15. (a) Where is the intervention of the Lord when wickedness occurs?; (b) Why does God seem indifferent?; (c) Why doesn't God address the affliction of the godly and punish the wicked?; and (d) Is God not obligated to uphold His own Law?
16. God used the Babylonians to punish or ravage the sinful nation of Judah.
17. True
18. (a) Habakkuk 2:9—Answers will vary. (God will punish those who have gained illegally and through unnecessary violence, protecting themselves from people like themselves or from people that they have victimized); (b) Habakkuk 2:12—Answers will vary. (God will punish those who have built their city spilling the blood of innocent people).

19. earth, filled, knowledge, glory, LORD, waters
20. Answers will vary.

Answer Key to Lesson 8
1. c
2. i
3. g
4. a
5. j
6. b
7. e
8. d
9. f
10. h
11. Calvin wanted to know, "How could a God of love sentence anyone to eternal punishment?"
12. holy
13. Carl convinced Calvin that: (a) God's judgment is true and (b) God's punishment is real.
14. He was: (a) persecuted, (b) plotted against, (c) maligned, and (d) imprisoned.
15. Jeremiah prophesied that God sees and will deal with it accordingly.
16. He was a (a) prophet and a (b) priest.
17. Answers will vary. (The Lord spoke to His chosen people about their sin in the beginning—the first time that they were wicked, but they did not listen, they did not hear, and they did not obey).
18. False
19. all, LORD, early, speaking, heard not, called, answered not, cast, out, all, brethren, whole
20. Answers will vary.

Answer Key to Lesson 9
1. f
2. j
3. g
4. h
5. i
6. a
7. e
8. c
9. d
10. b
11. (a) loneliness, (b) emptiness, (c) meaninglessness, and (d) suffering
12. craftsmen
13. (a) build houses; (b) plant gardens; (c) arrange marriages for their children; and (d) seek the peace and prosperity of the city of their captivity
14. words, God
15. d
16. Answers will vary.
17. True
18. deliverance, captivity
19. (a) "And ye shall seek me, and find me when ye shall search for me with all your heart" (Jeremiah 29:13); (b) Answers will vary.
20. Answers will vary to the first part of the question. The answer to the second part is "Jesus' role is to pay our sin-penalty by dying on the Cross."

Answer Key to Lesson 10
1. e
2. c
3. a
4. i
5. h
6. b
7. j
8. d

9. g
10. f
11. She put all of her faith in God.
12. His mom hoped that Dexter would accept Christ as his personal Lord and Saviour.
13. (a) root out, (b) throw down, (c) build, and (d) plant
14. passionate expressions, grief, Jeremiah
15. faith, beauty, ashes, city
16. rest
17. service
18. False
19. (a) "It is good that a man should both hope and quietly wait for the salvation of the LORD" (Lamentations 3:26); (b) Answers will vary.
20. Answers will vary.

Answer Key to Lesson 11
1. e
2. f
3. h
4. a
5. j
6. i
7. b
8. d
9. g
10. c
11. Should parents be held responsible for the wrong actions of their teenage children?
12. The elders felt that the Children of Israel had to suffer because of the sins of their parents.
13. ugly, serious
14. responsibility
15. guilt, punishment, own
16. b
17. False
18. True
19. (a) "Behold, all souls are mine; as the soul of the father, so also the soul of the son is mine: the soul that sinneth, it shall die"; (b) Answers will vary.
20. Answers will vary.

Answer Key to Lesson 12
1. g
2. f
3. i
4. a
5. h
6. j
7. d
8. c
9. b
10. e
11. Greg wanted to help others who needed Jesus as their Lord and Saviour, too.
12. repent, compassion, justice, mercy
13. righteousness, repentance, spirituality, worship, home life, and politics
14. (a) God called Zechariah to proclaim His Word to the remnant; and (b) to point out and explain the consequences of their sin by calling them to repentance and obedience.
15. God called Zechariah (a) to inspire the people and encourage them to finish rebuilding the temple; (b) restore the people's recognition of God in government; (c) restore the people's faith and hope during their period of despair; (d) bring the people back to true order and worship of God; and (e) repent from their sinful worship of idol gods.
16. b
17. True

18. (a) It was time to get right with God; (b) renew their relationship with God; (c) brush off the discouragement; (d) pull themselves together; and (e) obey God's commands.
19. "And oppress not the widow, nor the fatherless, the stranger, nor the poor; and let none of you imagine evil against his brother in your heart."
20. Answers will vary.

Answer Key to Lesson 13
1. g
2. e
3. j
4. f
5. i
6. h
7. d
8. a
9. b
10. c
11. Pastor Long prayed that: (a) his new church would be a community of faith; (b) he would learn the personal stories of his congregants; (c) the congregation would show compassion toward one another; (d) his church would strengthen and challenge each other; (e) the congregants would bear each other's burdens and help the oppressed, the fatherless, and the poor; and (f) his leadership would bring others to Christ.
12. (a) Malachi confronted the people for their neglect of the temple; and (b) for their false worship in the temple.
13. (a) making wrong sacrifices; (b) disobeying the laws of God; and (c) mistreating the poor and downtrodden
14. d
15. (a) rejecting the worship of God; (b) social wrongs and disorder in the home; and (c) robbery in the service of the temple through tithing
16. repetitious ceremonial prayers, sinful
17. (a) God will send a messenger; (b) the Lord will appear suddenly in his temple; (c) the Lord will come as the messenger of the covenant; and (d) the messenger of the covenant will be the one the people are hoping for
18. True
19. judgment, swift witness, sorcerers, adulterers, false swearers, oppress, widow, fatherless, stranger, fear, hosts
20. Answers will vary.

EMPOWERMENT THROUGH CHRIST

Since 1970, UMI has been developing quality Sunday School lessons especially designed to empower African American children, youth, and adults for successful Christian living.

Young people are empowered to overcome all obstacles. Teachers are given the tools to inspire them to learn about and follow Jesus Christ.

1-800-860-8642
urbanministries.com

Be an effective teacher!

Strategies for Teaching African
American Adults
Item No: 6-9705
ISBN: 1-932715-80-0
Paperback, $14.95

Strategies for Teaching African
American Children
Item No: 6-9704
ISBN: 1-932715-79-7
Paperback, $14.95

New from UMI, the Teaching for Spiritual Growth series will equip educators with the tools
needed to successfully teach and communicate with African American students of all ages.
You'll discover:

- How history and heritage impact teaching and understanding

- Learning styles at different stages of maturity

- Elements of good lesson plans and methods

- Tactics for organizing a multilevel Christian Education program

Order today! Urbanministries.com or 800.860.8642

UMI

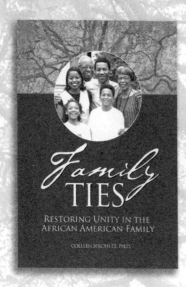

Family TIES

RESTORING UNITY IN THE AFRICAN AMERICAN FAMILY

To move from struggle to liberation, the African American family is in need of a vision. *Family Ties* addresses the critical need to reconnect the Black family with the type of unity that has historically been at the root of its strength. This book deals with the struggles that come against the family, such as racism, classism, economic uncertainty, and a lack of spiritual and ethnic identity.

Family Ties contains vignettes from a collection of Bible families, paired with an inside look at today's African American family. Each chapter illustrates timeless values by presenting background information on the historical context of Bible families, which gives guidance for today's African American families.

Order today! 800.860.8642 or www.urbanministries.com

Great for: Bible Study Groups/Vacation Bible School/Retreats/Book Clubs/ Family-Based Bible Studies/Church School Electives

Student book: $9.99, softcover
Item No. 6-5810, ISBN: 1-932715-69-X

Leader's guide: $8.99, softcover
Item No. 6-5820, ISBN: 1-932715-68-1

Student workbook: $2.99, softcover
Item No. 6-5850, ISBN: 1-932715-70-3

Kit (all three books): $17.99
Item No. 6-5840

URBAN OUTreach
FOUNDATION

42nd Annual
Urban Outreach Conference for Christian Education and Leadership Development

October 4-7, 2006

Who should attend?
**Christian Educators • Sunday School Teachers
Superintendents • Pastors • Lay Leaders
Seminarians • Biblical Students**

If you're interested in Christian Education or growing your Sunday School, you don't want to miss this conference!

**Newly renovated Double Tree Hotel
Oakbrook, IL
(just 20 minutes from O'Hare Airport)**

For 2007 date, please visit our website

Register Early To Save!!!

**Visit our website at www.urbanoutreach.net
or call 1-800-413-2214 for more information.**

THE GUARDIAN LINE

JOE & MAX • CODE • GENESIS 5 • THE SEEKERS

COMING YOUR WAY
SEPTEMBER 2006!

Not what you think, more than you expect!

GUARDIAN
A UMI COMPANY

www.TheGuardianLine.com